IMPROV QUILTING

DANCING
WITH THE
WALL

IMPROV QUILTING

IRENE
RODERICK

Interweave

Interweave®

An imprint of Penguin Random House LLC
penguinrandomhouse.com

Printed in Malaysia

3 5 7 9 10 8 6 4 2

ISBN 978-0-59333-141-5

Packaged by BlueRed Press Ltd. 2022
Designed by Insight Design Concepts Ltd.
Type set in Montserrat and Bebas

Photo credits
All photography by the author except:
Amanda Ruden—pp. 96 (BR),
Donna Blalock—pp. 96 (TL),
Marilyn Knepp—pp. 96 (BL),
Mary Hogan—pp. 95 (BR),
Petra Reeves—cover, pp. 4, 18 (BL), 101, 105, 111, 113, 115, 117, 121, 134, 135 TL, 136, 137, 138, 139, 140, 141 (BOTH), 143 (BOTH), 144, 147, 150, 151, 152, 154, 156, 157, 158, 159, 160, 162, 163, 164, 165, 166, 167, 168, 169, 170, 171, 172, 173, 174, 175, 176

I dedicate this book to my four sons, Marshall, Travis, Taylor, and Max for their lifelong patience and support.

Measurements
I dance in Imperial measurements, not metric!

Some of the metric equivalents need rounding up or down.

If you cannot work in Imperial, use this chart to see the exact equivalents, and round to a figure you can sensibly measure.

Metric Conversion Chart

inch	mm
1/8	3.175mm
1/4	6.35mm
3/8	9.525mm
1/2	12.7mm
5/8	15.875mm
3/4	19.05mm
7/8	22.225mm
1	25.4mm
2	50.8mm
3	76.2mm
4	101.6
5	127mm

Contents

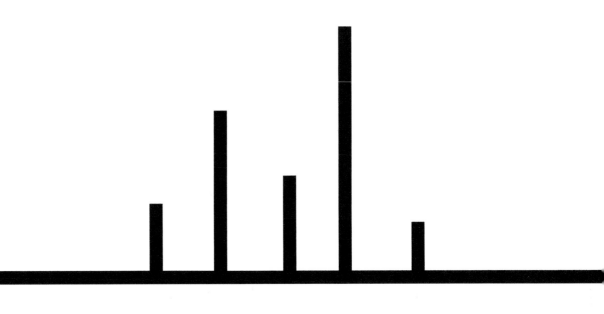

INTRODUCTION

One morning I was working in my studio on a new quilt. I had seen a painting on the internet composed entirely of blue and white wonky stripes and decided to try to make a quilt similar to it. I pieced together strips of indigo and white scraps into a small piece of fabric about 7in x 6in and placed it in the center of my design wall. I sewed together a few more pieces of blue and white-striped fabric. Then I made some diagonal stripes. I cut some into pieces and sewed them back together in different configurations. I made them in varying sizes. I placed them on the design wall next to the first one, stepped back, and was intrigued by the patterns they were making.

I kept adding more pieces until I felt it had lost momentum: I was no longer having fun. It wasn't going anywhere. It was just a bunch of blue and white stripes. Frustrated, I went to my scrap bin and pulled out some leftovers from a previous quilt, and stuck them up on the wall. These were large dark blue pieces from which half-circles had been cut. Next to the stripes, these created an interesting design element. I continued for a while longer until I once again decided it just wasn't working. So, back to the bin.

This time I pulled out a small quarter circle of bright yellow. I walked over, placed it into the design and stepped back. As I looked at the wall, the hairs on the back of my neck stood on end—something had happened. Something unexpected. Something exciting. The wall had suddenly become activated: the colors, the shapes, the relationships between the patterns were in the exact place they needed to be. I had crossed a line into intuitive creativity that I had been trying to find over the past forty years of making art.

To keep a record, I started writing down each step of my process as I worked on this quilt and the next one. I soon realized I was dancing around my studio all day as I moved from the design wall, the cutting table, the sewing machine, the ironing board, and back to the wall. I would step back and study the design as I added each piece of fabric to decide what the next step would be. I listened to music while I worked—rock and roll, bluegrass, country, and reggae music—I was literally dancing all day! Dancing with the Wall was born.

This book invites you to dance through the overview of how I work, and then start your own dance. It introduces you to my process from the beginning of a quilt to the finishing touches. I'm giving you all the tools and information you need to begin your own quilt. Then I want to set you free to let your creativity and your voice begin to emerge through fearless, playful experimentation. I have no rules in my own work, and I want you to throw yours out as well. I use rulers to cut fabric, but sometimes not. I like the challenge of piecing my quilts entirely, but some designs may need to include appliqué. I sometimes need to draw a specific curve with disappearing ink. I use pins—a lot of pins. I add more colors. I take some out. There are no rules except to stop planning or overthinking. Relax, play, and see what happens. You *will* make mistakes: you *will* get frustrated. You'll decide that you can't do it. However, you *will* also experience joy, satisfaction, excitement, and decide it's all worth it after all!

Specifically for this book, I have designed a quilt comprised of most of the components I show you how to make in these pages. If you choose, you may make this quilt as a sampler piece to practice the components and engineering process. I have given instructions for a 60in x 70in (152cm x 178cm) quilt, and have also broken it down into two different 24in x 24in (61cm x 61cm) mini-quilts or pillow tops. These instructions are not intended as a pattern to follow, but more as a guide. I have included a diagram and dimensions: choose your own unique palette of prints and solids then give it a try.

Remember though, the real reason for the book is to be a guide for you to find your own creative voice through a process of letting go of all expectations, all plans, all patterns.

IMPROV QUILTING: WHAT IS IT?

Improvisational quilting means letting go of all expectations and preconceptions of what you are going to make.

Let your subconscious and creativity drive your process to a unique expression of your aesthetic sensibility. Relax, play, let it happen, and see what comes out. You may love it: you may hate it (at first), but put it away for a week or two and then revisit it. You will like it much more—but above all, have fun and enjoy the process.

This method/process will work for any medium. Try it with painting, collage, printmaking, even creative writing!

The first thing to say is that improv is not easy. The process requires letting go of control—but at the same time remaining constantly thoughtful. Keep reminding yourself to get out of your own way and let it happen. Even if you are very accustomed to improvisational quilting, the process can be exhausting—but also very rewarding. It is an exciting process of discovery and invention.

IMPROV IS **NOT SLOPPY**

IMPROV IS **THOUGHTFUL** AND
CONSIDERED SPONTANEITY

STAY **RELAXED**, STAY **CONNECTED**,
STAY **ALERT**

LET **YOUR** CREATIVITY
DIRECT **YOUR** PROCESS

DON'T PLAN —
DON'T OVERTHINK

TRUST YOURSELF,
TRUST THE PROCESS

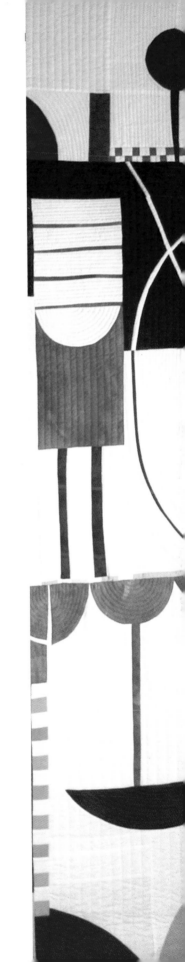

MY IMPROV ODYSSEY

I discovered quilting when I was searching online for a new, modern quilt. I had just moved into a tiny house and I needed a statement piece for my bed. Little did I know that the modern quilt was a "thing." The first quilt that caught my eye was a Denyse Schmidt minimal quilt. It was made from huge sections of bright red-orange and yellow-orange with small contrasting strips and pieces across the center. It looked like a contemporary painting and I was very intrigued. I started a deeper dive into what she was doing. My research inevitably led me to the quilts of Gwen Marston and Nancy Crow. I had never seen such beautiful, interesting work made from fabric, and I immediately decided I needed to explore this medium more thoroughly. I not only needed to explore—but I wanted a quilt similar to these for my own bed! But to possess one, I needed to make one.

I signed up for a beginners' quilting class and learned how to make a half-square triangle nine-patch quilt. To me, it was fascinating how the different fabrics being used by the other students created unique designs and effects. I was hooked. I started collecting books on contemporary quilting. I began learning every quilting technique. I made a double wedding ring quilt using plastic templates for son number three's wedding. I joined the Katje Quilt Shoppe "New Hexagon Millefiore Quilt-Along" kaleidoscope, fussy cutting, paper piecing, block of the month group on Facebook. I ordered sets of pre-cut fabric triangles in every solid color and sewed them together into a quilt I call "Prism." I did large-scale raw-edge appliqué for *Red Shoes*. I was hungry to learn it all. I started designing my own quilts and made some pretty awful messes as well, all in the name of learning.

A turning point in my practice occurred when the Modern Quilt Guild convention and exhibition, QuiltCon traveled to Austin in 2015. I saw a local news story on television showing some of the quilts on display. That weekend I made my way down to the conference and was blown away with the designs, techniques, and originality of these modern quilts. I watched every demonstration available and listened to every free lecture, even though not really understanding much of what I was seeing or hearing. I challenged myself to keep learning and to make a "modern" quilt to enter into the next QuiltCon

exhibition. The result was *Primarily Minions* (see opposite) and it was successfully juried into QuiltCon 2016.

It's important to let you know that I had no prior history with quilting. As I started to make quilts, I was completely unaware that there existed quilt rules and quilt police! No one in my family quilted: not my grandmothers, nor my aunts, or my mother. But what I do have is a long history of making art, painting in particular. I began painting when I received my first oil painting set at the age of ten; I earned a Bachelor of Fine Arts degree when I was forty-six, and four years later a Master's degree in Fine Arts at the age of fifty.

I have painted furniture, paintings, murals, and needlepoint designs. Because of my art background, I started building my quilts on a design wall in the same way I create paintings, but using fabric as a medium instead of paint. I started making improv quilts not realizing at the time that improv quilting is also a "thing." I now realize how lucky I am to have come to quilting after a lifetime of studying and making art. From the beginning of my quiltmaking practice, I have had a strong foundation of experience in making art without the hindrance of preconceptions about quilt rules. What constantly surprises me is how this new medium has opened a new way of working and thinking about my art. I have never experienced such freedom of creativity. Quilting has helped me discover my own artistic style and opened a new world of inspiration and excitement.

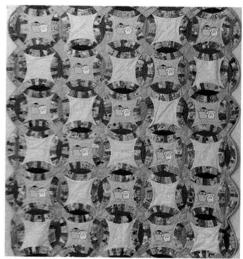

Double Wedding Ring *for Taylor*

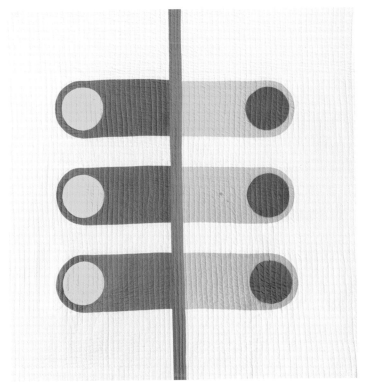

Primarily Minions *(QuiltCon 2016)*

Katje QuiltShoppe *(Millefiore)*

Lawn Pawns *(QuiltCon 2017)*

Red Shoes *(Raw edge appliqué)*

FINDING YOUR VOICE

Even after years of painting, I had not found a singular viewpoint or style that I would consider unique to my work. Dancing with the Wall enabled me to find that creative voice. My quilts are recognizable and distinctive because of the colors, shapes, and designs I use to make them. These come from my unique life experiences—my aesthetic sense is well embedded in my subconscious and specific, individual place in the world. As is yours. I cannot make your quilts and you cannot make mine. You don't need to have a degree in fine arts and you don't need a lot of experience taking classes in design or color theory. All you need is what is already in your head and heart.

We come from different places with different influences and different viewpoints. Because this process insists on letting go of all expectations and preconceptions, it becomes a discovery of the culmination of your background and knowledge. I always find it surprising to see what I make. When I delve deeper into the colors I have chosen or the design elements I have used, I can identify the influences behind these decisions. It may be something I've been looking at online, it may be something I've seen on TV, it may be something someone has said to me. It is probably a deep-set emotion that needs expression. I liken it to dreaming; I love the insight my work reveals about me, and how I feel about the world at that particular moment in my life.

Experience

Your quilting experience doesn't matter. This process is different from any other quilting you may have done. Improv quilting—especially the engineering—is not a simple process. It concerns weird shapes and seams. It involves high-level problem solving. It is also very rewarding. When you finish piecing your Dancing with the Wall project, you know that you can tackle any quilting challenge and be successful.

All you need is a sense of adventure and the willingness to discover something new about yourself and your skills. I find Dancing with the Wall the most challenging and rewarding form of making I've ever done, including painting, sculpture, beading, woodworking, printmaking, and needlepoint designing. Every new project is a chance for fresh discoveries.

Inspiration

It's not just a timeworn cliché that inspiration can be found anywhere and everywhere—it's the truth! You can look out your window right now and see something interesting. A new color in that dry, dead grass, or a shape between the window bars. Learn to look at the world in that microscopic way and see what is right in front of you.

Look at paintings, and prints, and quilts, and postcards that catch your eye. Is it the color? Probably. But dig deeper. Is it more than color? Do linear patterns draw your attention? Maybe it's all the curves in a flower. Pay attention to the moods that call to you. Do you love misty, pastel scenes? Are you mainly drawn to brightly colored images? The things you love are deeply embedded in you. You have developed your aesthetic preferences through your experiences. Maybe the love of your life proposed on a dark, cloudy day and you've felt safe and loved in foggy colors ever since. Maybe you were afraid of the clowns at the circus and you still shy away from bright reds.

Start noticing and collecting images that you love. When you are ready to start a new project, look through them, and then put them away. They are already in your mind and the ones you need in your piece will emerge as you work. Think of it as a similar phenomenon as dreams, with thoughts that reflect your circumstances, fears, joys, and that movie you watched and enjoyed all those years ago.

Tar marks in the street

Deck railing outside my window

Sunlight through my plants

Graffiti on a closed diner

SETTING
THE STAGE

TOOLS

Batting

Let's save this discussion for the quilting section (see p.97).

Camera/Phone

I know you have one and you will be taking photos of your work quite often. It is a wonderful tool to get a new perspective by seeing your piece smaller on the phone screen. If you are working in a small space, it may also be the best way to observe what you are doing.

Cutting Mat

Cover over all of your cutting table with a self-healing cutting mat. This will keep you from having to scoot your fabric around to keep it on the mat. I don't rely on the preprinted grids for measuring but prefer rulers for accuracy.

Cutting Table

As large and as flat as possible.

Design Wall

A large design wall is the most important tool in your quiltmaking. I insist mine be 7ft x 8ft (213cm x 244cm) minimum. If you don't have much room, hang batting over a closet door or across a wall. You absolutely need to see what you are making!

Fabric

One hundred-percent cotton is easiest to work with. You may use other fabrics such as linen and silk, but they are more difficult and may require stabilizers. I don't normally prewash my fabrics. I feel that the quality of contemporary fabrics has much improved and they do not shrink or release dyes as in the past. However, if I know a quilt will be heavily used and washed many times, such as a baby quilt, I do take the extra time to prewash all the fabric to shrink it and thoroughly clean it of added chemicals. I am aware, though, that most of my quilts will not be thrown into a washing machine but instead will hang on a wall.

Iron/Ironing Board

Use the biggest you can fit in your space. I find woolen pressing mats useful for flat pressing. I have two sizes: the small one is out all the time for daily jobs, while the big one fits onto my ironing board for larger jobs.

Pins and Needles

I love the glass-head pins that don't melt when I iron over them. I also like the long ones because they stay in place better and are easier to work with.

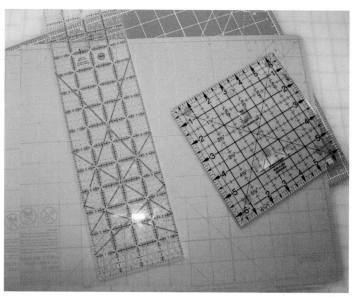

Rotary Cutters

I have all three metric sizes of rotary cutters: 28mm, 45mm, and 60mm (1.1in, 1.77in, and 2.36in).

I love the smaller one for tight curves, the medium one for general cutting, and the large one is fantastic for cutting those WOF (width of fabric) strips.

Rulers

Yes, I use quilting rulers for many tasks. I find them useful for squaring up components, cutting strips for checkerboards, and faster cutting in general. I love my 6.5in x 24in (16.5cm x 61cm) ruler, but also use my 4in x 14in (10cm x 35.5cm), and 6.5in x 6.5in (16.5cm x 16.5cm) rulers for smaller jobs.

Scissors and Seam Rippers

I have numerous scissors in all sizes, and seam rippers at every station, including near my comfy chair for sit-down jobs.

Sewing Machine

Any good machine that sews a straight stitch will do—no need for fancy frills and whistles.

Starch

Any starching agent helps keep wonky pieces under control and makes your construction much easier. I use cheap liquid starch mixed 50/50 with water. It works just fine and is completely odor free.

Tailor's Clapper

Makes thick and pesky seams behave better. A clapper is a traditional tailor's tool made from a piece of hardwood about 2in thick and 3in wide (5cm x 7.5cm), and shaped for easy handling. It is used to get flat, crisp seams. To use it, press the seam well and immediately place the clapper on top of it. The wooden clapper will absorb the moisture and hold in heat with just the right amount of pressure for a nice, flat seam.

Thread

I suggest 40 or 50-weight cotton or polyester thread for piecing. My machine loves 40-weight cotton in the top and 50-weight in the bobbin or it fusses at me. I will discuss threads for quilting in the quilting section later in the book (see p.98).

Tracing Paper

A nice 14in x 17in (35.5cm x 43cm) pad works in most cases. I use it for engineering those difficult sections.

Writing/Drawing Implements

Heat-sensitive ink, disappearing ink, chalk: all work. Whatever your favorite marking implement is, use it. Please don't get it confused with a regular ink pen or use a pencil. Pencil can actually break down fabric over years and you don't want to be erasing when your quilt is finally done.

> *I am not a tool snob— whatever you can afford will work just fine*

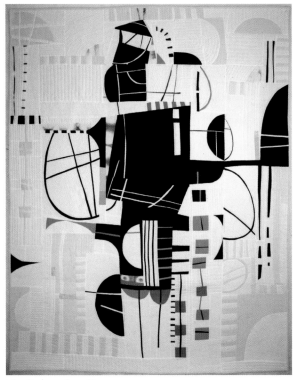

Mr. Bojangles, Dance

Empty Speech Bubbles

DESIGN

This is a big topic!

I can't design your quilt for you. As a matter of fact, if you've been reading carefully, you know that you're not supposed to be designing your quilt either. You are using an intuitive process to make your quilt. It is in no one's hands but in your subconscious mind. What does that leave us to discuss? The following thoughts are some considerations you might want to think about based on your own aesthetic sensibility:

I would like to talk a little about the first three of these questions because

> *Is your style figurative or more of an overall pattern?*
> *What is the figure/ground relationship you most use?*
> *What is the scale/size you prefer to work in?*
> *Do you like symmetry or asymmetry?*
> *Are you most comfy with big, graphic patterns?*
> *Do you prefer tiny, intimate piecing in quilts?*
> *Are you a calm, sedate, sophisticated person?*
> *Are you a crazed troublemaker?*
> *Are you political and like to make work with a purpose?*
> *Are you interested in creating new visual patterns?*
> *Do you need to be grounded with representational images?*
> *Do you love abstraction?*

they are universal design considerations and not based on individual aesthetics. These design elements are also terms you will encounter in art and design discussions and are good to know.

Figurative or overall pattern

A figurative design is often a "figure" on a background. This is not the same as representational art, in that it is not necessarily a realistic or recognizable representation of an object, person, or animal. The difference is that the main design elements in a figurative design create a coherent structure that stands out against a field or background. Most of my quilts such as *Mr. Bojangles, Dance* fall into this category.

An overall pattern organizes the space into repeating units of shapes or forms that fall across the surface more equally in color and relevance. My quilts *Dancing With Belle* and *Bonnie Raitt* are prime examples of an overall pattern.

Figure/ground relationship

The figure/ground relationship in a design can also be defined as foreground/background or positive space/negative space. It is important to realize that negative space is as important as positive space in creating your quilt. Those empty areas have as much significance as the filled areas. In quilting, these areas can be spaces to showcase your quilting skills. While you are designing, it is always a good idea to keep in mind that the fabric you are seeing on your wall is only the first step. The actual quilting is another important design element and should be taken into consideration as well. The large areas of white in *Empty Speech Bubbles* are activated by the thin quilting lines.

Size—bed sizes

The size of your quilt is not as random as that of a painting, say, unless you are intentionally making a wall piece. If you want a quilt to fit on a particular bed, you need to make it large enough to cover it, but not so large that it falls onto the floor. If you are making a quilt for your college dorm-bound student, it needs to fit those built-in twin beds. If you are making a baby floor pad, remember that it needs to be easily thrown into a washing machine. Common quilt (not bed) sizes are:

Baby/Crib	36in x 52in (91cm x 132cm), or for a floor pad 30in x 40in (76cm x 102cm)
Lap	50in x 65in (127cm x 165cm)
Single/Twin	70in x 90in (178cm x 229cm)
Double	85in x 108in (216cm x 274cm)
Queen	90in x 108in (229cm x 274cm
King	110in x 108in (279cm x 274cm)

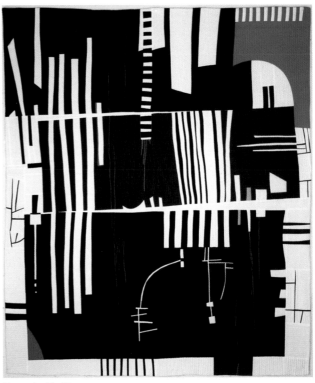

Bonnie Raitt

Dancing With Belle

COLOR

I'm not going to regale you with an essay on color. There are many, many, books and websites that you can read. If you look at my quilts, you can see that most use only a few colors. Even then, my use of color is intuitive. I start a quilt without a specified palette. As I work and need to add a color, I'll often have an idea of the perfect fit. I then pick out a stack of possibilities and try them out one by one. Then I narrow the stack down to three or four that seem to work. Out of those, the perfect one seems to jump out at me. I do this every time I decide I need to add another color.

Color, though, is not the end all. The end all is "value." There's an old saying: "color has all the fun but value does all the work." That is true. Try to use a variety of values (light, medium light, mid-tones, medium dark, dark) to make your quilts sing! Use the black and white filter on your phone to quickly and easily clarify values.

All that is good to know, but . . .

Colors don't behave

They are shifty little fellows. Colors change depending on who they are hanging with— they have implied meanings.

These meanings can be:

Holidays
Eras
Memories
School colors
And especially emotions!

Secret, Hidden Meanings

Holidays

Eras

Memories

and espacially Emotions

You need to know these seven important things when using color:

IT'S COMPLICATED: IT'S NOT TANGIBLE
IT'S A FIGMENT OF YOUR IMAGINATION

YOU CAN'T TOUCH IT, BUT YOU CAN "FEEL" IT

IT CHANGES ALL THE TIME
IT'S RELATIVE TO EVERY COLOR IT IS AROUND

IT HAS VALUES; IT'S NOT SCARY
BUT IT DEMANDS RESPECT AND CLOSE CONSIDERATION

CHARTREUSE IS MY FAVORITE COLOR
I CALL IT "IRENE GREEN"

PUCE IS A DARK BROWNISH RED
I CAN NEVER REMEMBER THIS COLOR

COLOR HAS ALL THE FUN, BUT VALUE DOES ALL THE WORK

SEMIOTICS

This is the study of signs and symbols. A sign or symbol is anything that communicates a meaning, whether intentional or not. In our everyday environment, octagons are indicative of stop signs. Concentric circles are targets. Triangles can represent trees or mountains. Parallel wavy lines often invoke water. There are many shapes and colors that remind us of actual objects. The human brain wants to define what we see in recognizable forms.

There is nothing wrong with using signs and/or symbols in your work. I want you to be aware that they are there and whether they are intentional or not, they make a statement to the viewer. It's fun to use five parallel lines to create a music staff. It's fun to make black and white stripes to indicate a piano keyboard. You may want to use triangles and wavy lines to make a landscape quilt. Remember though, there might

be some signs you want to avoid. For example, targets can be circular, or square, or triangular, and are very visually strong in a composition, pulling all the attention away from more subtle areas. Arrows are recognizable and directional. Are you really pointing? A checkerboard is a wonderful design element, but also draws visual attention. There's nothing wrong with doing any of that: know that shapes and colors have power, so use them intelligently and with intention.

In my own work, I try very hard to find shapes and colors that stand only as abstractions. Invariably, observers try to find images and point them out. If I see anything in my design that is easily defined as an animal or object, I will change it. I have had observers find birds, animals, pianos, people, and robots in my quilts. Once I see them, I can never un-see them and will probably fold that quilt and store it away—forever.

Tree or lollipop?

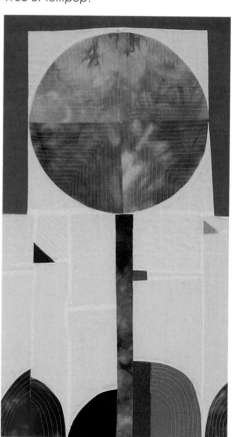

Houses?

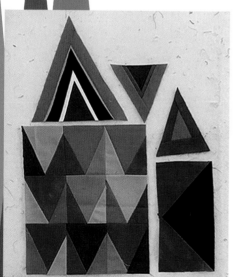

Dueling pianos?

22

DESIGN SPACE

If at all possible, I suggest you carve out a dedicated quilting/sewing space in your home. This is a space where you can set up your sewing machine and your quilting tools for easy access—an area you can close off for privacy and quiet. If you don't have the luxury of such a space, a corner in your bedroom with a piece of batting attached to the wall or thrown over the closet door will work just fine. You may need to be just as creative with your space as you are with your quilts!

An essential part of my space is a design wall. I need it to be at least 7–8ft (213cm x 244cm) tall and 6–7ft (183cm x 213cm) wide. I make it of ¾in thick construction foam board that comes in a 4ft x 8ft (122cm x 244cm) panel and can be attached to the wall with double-stick tape or a single big-head nail in each corner. If you don't have the wall space for an attached design wall, the foam board can be cut to as generous a size as your space can accommodate and be propped against the wall. You can store it behind or under your bed even with your quilt design in progress.

Pin each piece to the board and it will stay in place. The ¾in thickness handles all lengths of pins and secures the pins in place. I like to cover my board with white batting or flannel, because my fabric components will stick to it without pins. I attach the flannel to the foam substrate with t-pins so that I can easily replace it when it gets covered with errant threads and dirty spots.

I use white batting as a covering on my wall because many of my quilts are figurative with light colored backgrounds. The white keeps my colors bright and keeps my design clear. I find that gray design board coverings (especially the ones with grids), dull my colors by ghosting through the fabric and also disturb my creativity with all those even, parallel lines inviting me to line up all the elements.

When you are working on your quilt design, after you are about two-thirds done, mark out a boundary on your design wall in off-white masking tape or thin strips of black ribbon or fabric. Then add about 4in on all sides to accommodate for the shrinkage that takes place while sewing it all together.

TIP:
Everything on the design wall interacts with your quilt design. Keep extra components on a nearby table, not on the wall

CUE THE MUSIC...

LET'S
START

DANCING

BUILDING: DESIGNING YOUR QUILT

I have talked about improvisational quilting and a little about how I design my quilts. Let's now dive into what the process actually entails and how to get started.

This is how it all begins. This is what it's all about! This is when you let go of all expectations and all plans or ideas you may have. This is the play part! There are no rules: get out of your own way and let your intuition and creativity emerge. This is when you start to trust yourself—this is when you start to trust the process. This is when your own creative voice takes over.

This book is about giving you the tools and tips to discover what you can create. Everything you need to make is already in you. All you need to do is relax and let it come out.

I want you to quit thinking—but remain thoughtful. This process is not about doing shoddy, throw-stuff-at-the-wall, sort of work. This process is about looking and reacting. This process is about finding out what you can do if you let your subconscious and intuition take the lead. Anyone can take a bunch of scraps and sew them together randomly. But only *you* can make *your* quilt. Only you have your experiences, your sense of aesthetics, your way of looking, and being in the world.

Let's get started! I discovered over the making of many quilts that I use the same kinds of elements in all my work. They are like blocks in traditional quilting but not square and not all similar or repetitive. I call them components. I think of them as the structures I can rely on to make interesting interactions of color and shapes, including negative space. I didn't create the components to make the quilts: I looked at the quilts I had made and discovered that these were in every quilt. I use them over and over in different ways as the bones or framework on which to build. Compare it to building a house: every house has walls, doors, windows, and a roof, but there are millions of types of houses. I start with these basic structural components and then add my "furnishings" to them. You will discover your favorite components. You will design your own shapes and combinations based on your personal aesthetic.

It is okay to have an intention for a piece. Often, when I'm starting a new quilt, I set up a challenge for myself: I'll decide that I want to try to create a feeling of movement, or I may want to see if I can make a quilt that resembles a charcoal drawing. If I'm not feeling any particular inspiration, I may look online at artwork or go through my folder of inspiration images. Mostly though, I look around the studio and grab whatever attracts my attention. I don't give it much thought. Just this is a fun shape (or color, or left-over component) and place it in the center of my design wall. I have no idea at this point what my quilt will look like—I am not concerned about a finished concept. I just start with a single piece in the center, nothing else in my head. Always though, I have a tingling sensation in the pit of my stomach. With each beginning there's the fear that it won't work this time: that what I make will be awful. It's fear of the unknown. Even after making over a hundred quilts, it never fails to show up when I begin a new project. It is also the excitement of a fresh beginning. The excitement of the unknown. It's normal. Embrace it!

PLAY PLAY PLAY

Start by clearing your design wall—and remove any clutter or remnants of the last project from your cutting table. Then begin with a single component in the center of your wall. This first step can be a wonkily cut piece of fabric in a favorite color or print. It can be a left-over component from a prior quilt. It can be something sitting in the scrap pile that seems interesting.

Now it's time to start dancing.

Step back a few paces and study your component. Do you like the color? Is it interesting? Does it suggest what it needs next? Don't overthink. There's not a lot to see at this point. If it's a simple, solid piece of fabric, it might want something inserted into it. It might need a different color to play with in the next piece. If it has shapes or lines already in it, do those elements call for a following component to extend or open them up? If nothing comes to mind, make another component and place it on the wall next to the first.

Audition the second component in more than one location to see where it wants to go. I love to find the weirdest place to try a new element: in many cases, that's the place it wants to live. We see the world in the same ways on television or in graphics all over the city, and in magazines. We are accustomed to particular combinations of colors and arrangements on a page. Break those traditions. The idea is not to throw out all the rules, but to try something new. How can you rethink how you normally see things? Can you tweak a concept or mess with it? You won't know until you try. Soooo ... try that component in an unexpected place. It's okay to put it back in the place you originally thought it should go. That's where it might need to be. Put it in place and leave it there! Forever!

Repeat

Step back and make new components and place them on the wall one at a time until you get about five to eight pieces in your design. This is when the design starts to have an opinion of what it wants next. A long sit-down in front of it over a cup of tea or coffee with an open mind is the perfect time to "listen." When I'm asked to talk about how I make a particular quilt, I have no answer. I don't know how or why I make the decisions I make when I make them. Even when I look back at some of my quilts I think, "What was I thinking? That's crazy!" And that's what I love about this process. It often feels magical.

Keep going. Each step is a new decision.

Step back again and study your composition. What's next? Don't tell it: let it tell you. Trust your instincts. I don't want your head saying, "I'm going to make a triangle here and then I will balance it with another triangle over there and another over there." I don't want you thinking "I need to put in some yellow here because It's going to balance the flock of yellow geese that are going to fly across the top of my finished quilt." I want you to study the design on the wall and walk to your cutting table and pick up what your hand goes to and use it. Look carefully at what you've done. Respond with another component or a piece of fabric you find. Audition it in more than one location, find where it wants to go and leave it there. Do it again and again. Use the components as your building blocks.

Possible beginnings

You can start with a piece of fabric in a color that you love. This piece (1) was a leftover from an earlier project. I then added another piece of fabric (2) and started playing with little bits in the same colors off my cutting table.

This red and white component (3) is also a leftover from a prior project, *She's Lost Control Again*. I added a red and white strip and a skinny-line log cabin (4) as the next steps.

1
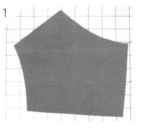

2
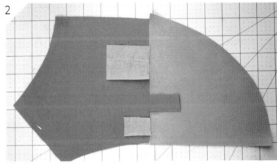

3
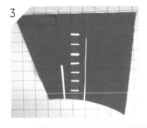

4
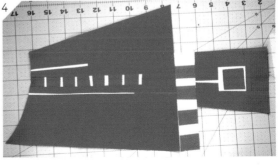

Document the process

After you get five or more components on the wall, take a photo—I do it on my phone—to document your process. When I had cats, they loved to sneak into the studio and destroy everything on my design wall. The photos taken at every step enabled me to replace the components without having to remember where they had formerly lived. You might think "it might be better or different if I put them up in new places," but because you have carefully considered each step and have already decided the components are where they want to be, don't rethink your decisions. You will make many more quilts and make many more different decisions. Finish this one, and then start another.

Dancing In Pomegranate
Perimeter line added to clarify the edges of the final quilt.
Do this about two-thirds of your way into the design process.

Adding a perimeter

Continue making components, placing them on the wall, leaving them alone until you think you are about half to three-quarters done. You have been working from the center out and now need to delineate the edges of your piece. You should now have a good idea of the finished size of your quilt. Using either a neutral-colored masking tape or very thin strips of black fabric, mark the outer perimeter of your finished quilt. Please don't use a green or blue painter's tape, because that distinctive tape becomes a visual part of your piece. I also want to advise you to take everything off your design wall that is not part of the quilt. Take the extra components hanging off to the side and place them on a table nearby instead of the wall. Everything on the design wall influences how you see your design. With a clean wall and the outline, you will have a clearer vision of how to proceed.

Now that you have an outer edge, you can start working from the outside edge toward the center design. You can see how the corners are working and what they need. Instead of continuing into an unknown, undelineated space, you now have a destination to work toward.

It is very difficult to teach someone how to be creative. There are no quilt police here. Your mother is not standing over you. I'm not standing over you. There are no rules. It's only fabric. There's plenty more in your stash. There may not be that exact fabric, but there are others that work and open new ways of thinking.

When you outline the perimeter of your quilt as you work, use only off-white masking tape or skinny black strips of fabric or ribbon. If you use colored tape, that color will interfere with how you see the colors in your piece

MY TOOLS: THE COMPONENTS

Components are my tools. They are the shapes and combinations that I use to create all my quilts. Traditional quilts are made of blocks that can be different colors and turned in different ways, but are usually square to easily fit together. Components are my blocks except that they aren't necessarily square or fit together easily.

The following components can be manipulated as to size, shape, or color to suit the quilt you are building on the wall.

My components aren't necessarily your components. You can design your own from shapes that appeal to you. Look around and find simple forms that you think would make fun components and make them for your unique quilt.

I don't use every kind of component in every quilt: I choose my components as I build my quilt, one at a time. Some quilts will only have skinny lines and curves, while others will be primarily stripes and squares.

Neat components make for a clearer vision of what is actually there

YOU DO NOT NEED TO USE EVERY COMPONENT IN YOUR QUILT— ONLY USE THEM AS A WAY TO DEVELOP YOUR DESIGN

AS YOU TAKE EACH STEP AND STUDY WHAT'S ON THE DESIGN WALL, CHOOSE ANY COMPONENT THAT TAKES YOUR DESIGN IN THE DIRECTION IT WANTS TO GO

IT MAY WANT A STRIPED STRIP OR IT MAY NEED A BIG CURVED PIECE

SOMETIMES A LONG, THIN STRIP OF A SOLID COLOR CAN LEAD YOU IN A NEW DIRECTION

PLAY!

NO PLANNING AHEAD ALLOWED!

In the following pages I'll show you how to make the components I use in all of my quilts. They are:

Lines (pp. 32–37)
Skinny and otherwise
Alligator skin/Tree bark
Antennae

Concentric skinny lines
Half circles
Embedded strips
Skinny lines across
curved pieces
Wave curves

Stripes (pp. 38–41)
Strips
Tips
Other things to do with
stripes

Triangles (pp. 60–67)
Half square triangles
Isosceles triangles
Log cabin triangles
Skinny line triangles

Squares (pp. 42–47)
Checkerboards
Log cabin blocks

Stars (pp. 68–69)

Curves (pp. 48–59)
Quarter circles
Adding cogs

Bits and slabs (pp. 70–71)
Scraps
Big pieces of fabric

Above: Happy Hair, Crazy Legs

Examples of quilts using components.

Right: Me 'N Morg

Opposite page;
Mr. Bojangles, Dance

Lines

Skinny and otherwise

So, skinny lines: the best component ever!

Everyone loves them. They can be straight or curved. They can stand alone, or adorn another shape, or group themselves into skinny stripes.

Skinny lines are very easily made.

Step 1   For a line narrower than ¼in, cut a strip of fabric ¾in wide to start with. This makes it easier to sew and press.

Step 2   Sew onto another fabric with a scant ¼in seam allowance. Press the seam allowance away from the skinny line so that you can see the sewing line.

Step 3   Now's the time to trim your skinny strip to size. If you want a line narrower than ¼in, trim to ³⁄₈in.

Step 4   Seam allowances for skinny strips after they are sewn love to be pressed to both sides.

Skinny lines can be made from striped strips (fig. 5 upper line). This also shows just how skinny skinny lines can be! Strip stripes can be made into skinny lines too. They are done the exact same way as regular thin lines (fig. 5 lower line).

Fig. 6 shows how the seam allowances for skinny lines should be pressed. Because there are many layers of seam allowance, letting them stay open reduces bulk.

One of my favorite ways to use skinny lines is to make them appear to stop part of the way through an element by making the strip partly of one color (fig. 7a) and partly of the background color (fig. 7b).

Skinny lines are beautiful in curves (fig. 8a) and create interest in other pieces. The combination of lines shown in fig. 8b are slightly radiating to express upward movement.

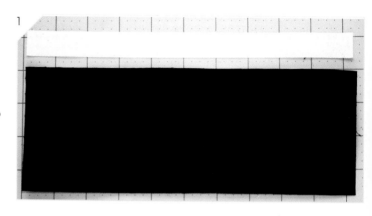

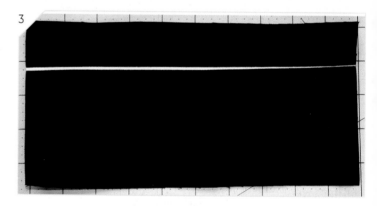

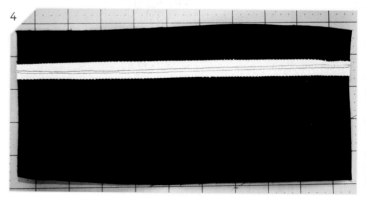

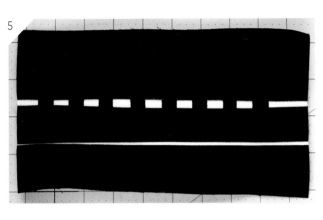

5

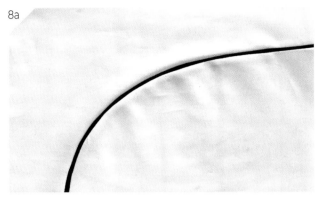

8a

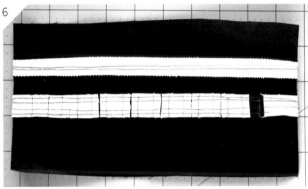

6

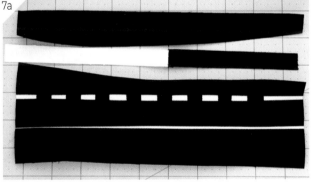

7a

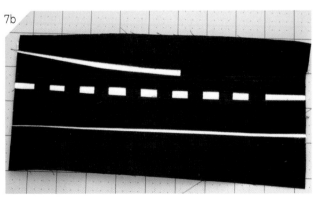

7b

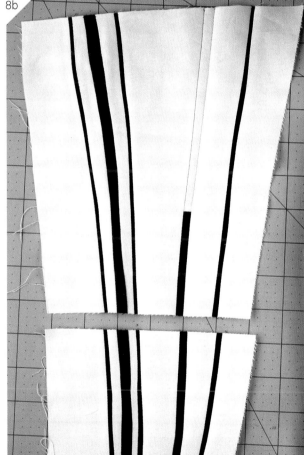

8b

LINES SKINNY AND OTHERWISE

Alligator skin/Tree bark

I call this component alligator skin or tree bark. You can also consider it a plaid if you use more than two colors.

Step 1   It is easily made by sewing thin strips onto wider strips.

Step 2   Sew together to make a component at least 1in larger than your desired finished size. You will lose width when you insert the cross lines.

Step 3   Slice the component into strips. Remember to consider seam allowance in the width you are cutting. You are inserting ⅛in lines and losing ½in in seam allowance.

Step 4   Insert thin strips of fabric (¾in minimum width) between your newly cut strips (figs. 4a and 4b).

Step 5   The seam allowances are very thick where all the lines intersect. You will need to starch and press them well—a tailor's clapper is very handy here to help flatten them a bit. Press the seam allowances open as well to decrease bulk.

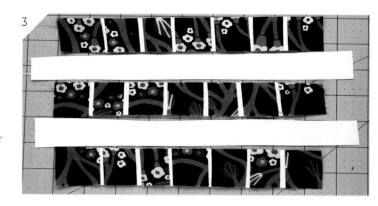

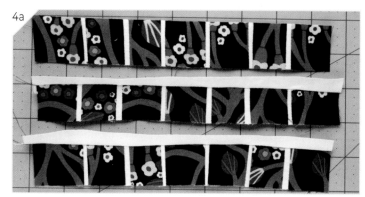

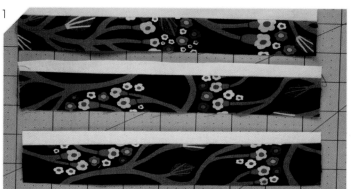

Step 6 Finish sewing the seam and then turn the piece upside down and sew the same seam from the other side to straighten the seam line (figs. 6a and 6b).

I like the way this component seems different when reversed from dark-to-light to light-to-dark (fig. 7).

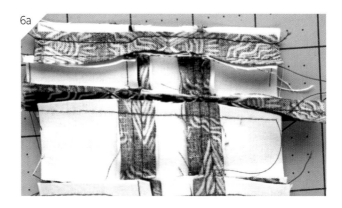

6a

6b

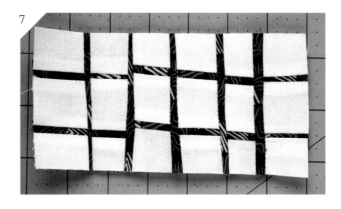

7

LINES ALLIGATOR SKIN / TREE BARK

Skinny-line antennae

Skinny lines are great for making many other interesting components. Even though they are narrow, they can fill a much larger space because they are dynamic. Antennae (the word comes from the old TV antennae we had on our roofs in the 1960s) are created by embedding a skinny line in a field of a background color, and then slicing and dicing various diagonals and dropping in more skinny lines (fig. 1).

Add as many or as few diagonals as you like. To get varying lengths, make short strips and add background fabric to each end (figs. 2 and 3).

I like to draw my diagonals before I cut them to ensure that they are not parallel. Some dip to the left, some to the right, but they are all different angles.

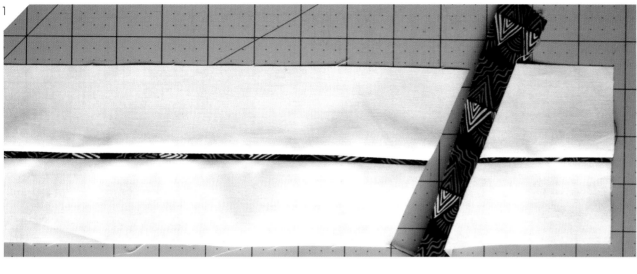

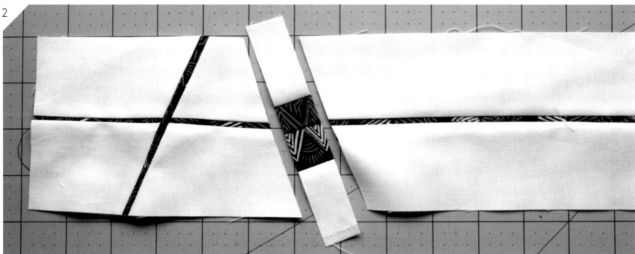

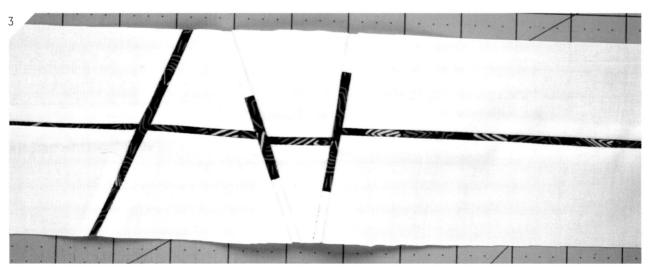

LINES SKINNY - LINE ANTENNAE

a

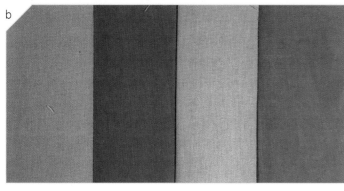

b

c

d

Stripes

Easy and versatile

Stripes are the base of many other great components—they are also easy to make and are effective by themselves.

Stripes can be made in different widths, different colors, and different configurations (figs. a–f). Just cut lengths of fabric and sew them together any way you want!

An easy way to make stripes is to cut strips from your fabric selvage-to-selvage in any width you want. If you want nice, straight lines, use your ruler (fig. g). If you prefer a wonky look, try cutting freehand. You can see the difference on fig. h, opposite above.

f

g

e

h

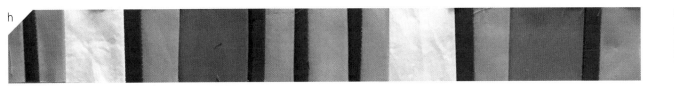

STRIPES STRIPS

To make a strip stripe

Step 1 Sew two strips of fabric together lengthwise and press open. These strips may be any width but must be the same length. Seam allowance can go any way you like. Now you have a long, narrow strip of two colors. Keep adding strips of fabric of the same length until you have a stripe you like. It can be several colors in varying stripe widths or two colors, as in this example.

Step 2 Fold your long strip in half and cut across the width.

Step 3 Sew these two together. Keep sewing and cutting in half until you get the stripe you want. For extra skinny lines, don't cut any width less than ¾in.

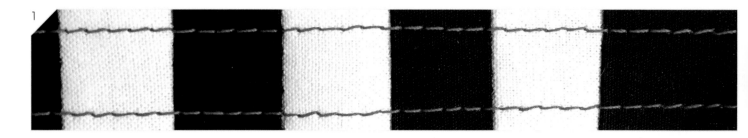

1

Stripe Tips

Stay stitching is your friend when you are making stripe strips, especially the thin ones. To stay stitch a stripe strip, press all of your seam allowances in the same direction then sew about 1/8in from the edges (above). It is worth the time and effort! When you sew them onto other pieces, you can enjoy not having pesky flipped or folded seam allowances on the back.

Iron into gentle curves

Need a gentle curved stripe strip? Use your iron to press in the curve. You can't make a sharp curve, but a gentle one works well. If you need a wonky skinny line, your iron is the perfect tool to use to un-straighten it.

2

Presser foot and skinny line sewing

Presser feet are designed to sew straight lines 1/4in apart. They don't like to sew skinny lines and will often fight you. If your machine has the ability to move your needle to the left, change your foot to one that is made for zigzag stitching and sew. Maybe your machine has a way to loosen the pressure of your foot. That works as well.

In my case with a machine that does neither, I just go slow to keep my skinny line as narrow as I want.

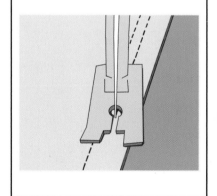

Other things to do with stripes!

Windows
Just add strips between striped strips (fig. 1 and 2).

Railroad track
Cut strip stripes into wide strips and insert another strip.

Beads
Beads aren't stripes but log cabins. Sew them into a strip and then slice in half. Insert a skinny strip to make into beads (fig. 4).

Squares

Checkerboards

The checkerboard is a component that demands your attention. The familiar, regular pattern can be used as a point of interest in your quilt. If you add black and white checkerboards to your design, they spark interest and make your other colors sing!

To make a checkerboard, I break my rule of "no rules." A true checkerboard needs to be cut with a ruler and in equal widths. Measure carefully, cut once.

Step 1 Cut the fabrics together for consistency and sew all seams with ¼in seams (fig. 1).

Step 2 Press all seams in the same direction. You want the seams to nest together when the strips are sewn to each other. This is another time I press seam allowances open. This will the reduce bulk, especially with smaller checkerboards.

Step 3 Cut cross-cuts the same width as the original strips.

Step 4 Flip every other strip upside down.

Step 5 This is another time I press seam allowances open. This is to reduce bulk, especially with smaller checkerboards.

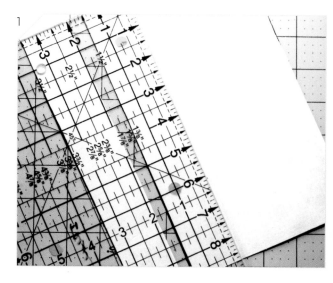

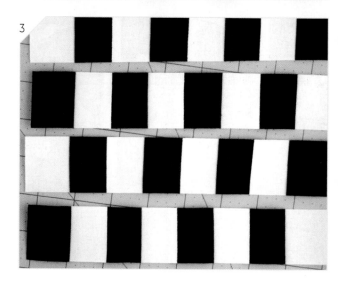

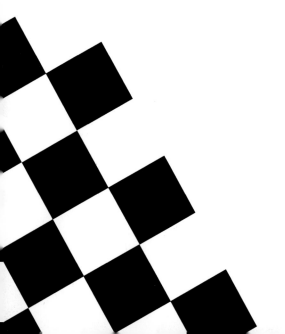

4

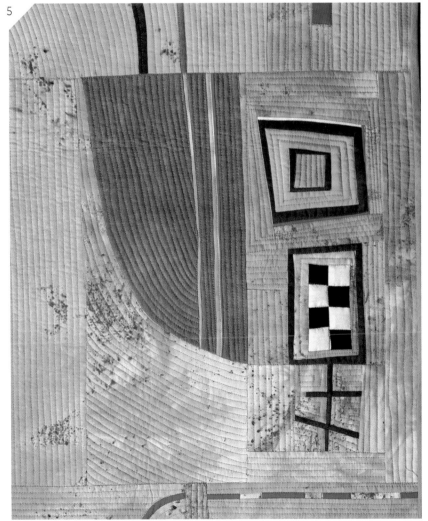

5

Left: Green Eggs and Ham
This demonstrates how black and white checkerboards make colors pop!

Log cabin blocks
The wonky skinny way

A log cabin block is a traditional block usually made with a red center block symbolizing the hearth of the cabin. But for our purposes, the colors are determined by the palette of your quilt.

I use many types of log cabin blocks in my quilts. I like to make them from skinny lines and put them on stems. Instead of a traditional very square block, I love to make them wonky with a lot of personality.

Step 1   To make your own, cut a center square between 1in square and 2in square. For the best result, don't make the center too small or too large. Because I want this one to be wonky, I have cut a trapezoid.

The next steps will be of another color or colors—they can be the same or different depending on the effect you want.

Step 2   Cut a strip of fabric longer than one side of your center and sew to the center. Wonkiness is achieved by making the sides slightly off-kilter.

Steps 3 This will create a diagonal edge that means the strips need to be cut at least 3in longer than you think you need to compensate for the diagonal. Repeat for the other three edges (figs. 3a–3d).

Step 4   To make this a skinny line log cabin, trim each side to 3/8in and press away from the skinny line, using starch and a clapper to get the seams as flat as possible (figs. 4a and 4b).

Step 5   The next round will be wide strips of a contrasting color. I make them all about 2in across and extra long to compensate for the diagonals of a wonky center (figs. 5a–5d).

1

2

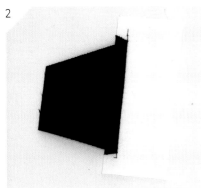

3a

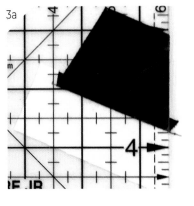

3b

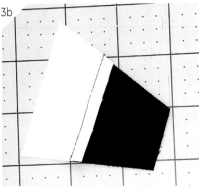

3c

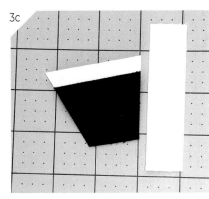

3d

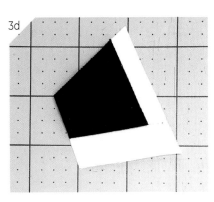

4a

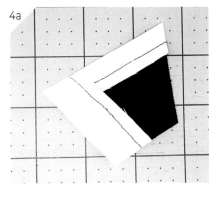

4b

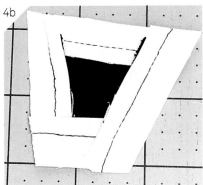

5a

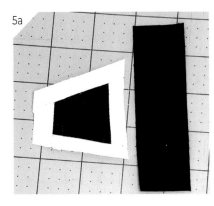

5b

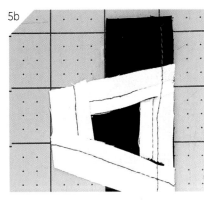

5c

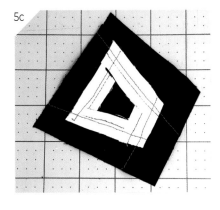

5d

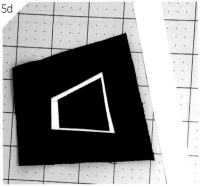

SQUARES LOG CABIN BLOCKS

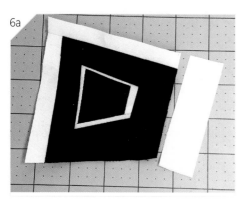

6a

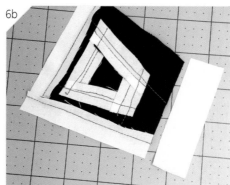

6b

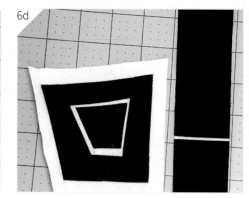

6d

Step 6   Do additional rounds until the log cabin is to your liking (figs. 6a–6c).

Step 7   To add a stem, insert a line into one side of the last round in a contrasting color (figs. 7a–7b).

7a

7b

Sewing sequence

You can see different approaches to log cabin blocks.
These can be as wonky as you like, but remember to
follow the correct—clockwise—sewing sequence, 1–13.

8

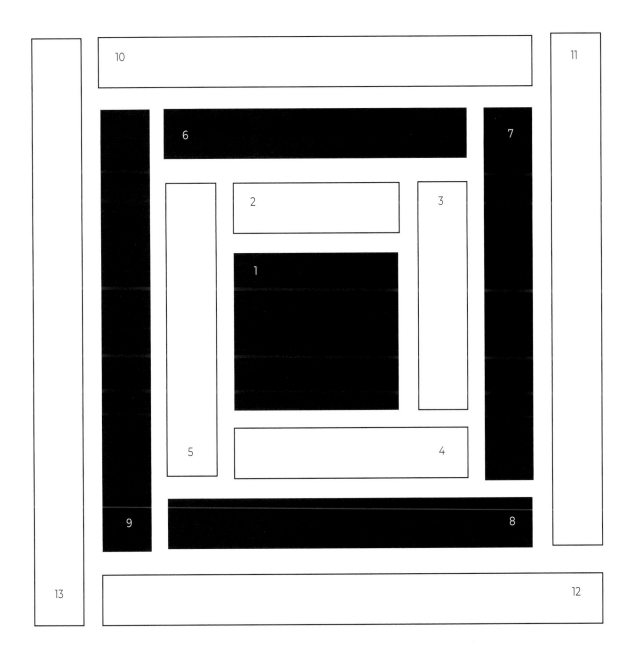

Curves
Are not scary!

They can seem scary—but they are simple to make.

Quarter circles

Step 1 To make improv curves, stack two equal-size pieces of fabric. If you are using print fabrics, both should be face up. Cut the curve through both fabrics (figs. 1a and 1b).

Step 2 Using the pie piece of one of the fabrics and the outside piece of the other, flip the pie piece at the curviest part of the curve and match edges, right side together (figs. 2a and 2b).

Step 3 Eyeball the two fabric curves to be as close to the center as possible. Place a pin at that center point where the fabrics meet.

Step 4 Continue to pin every ¾in in both directions, matching edges. Note that the ends will not line up.

When the curves are cut together, there is no built-in seam allowance. This causes the ends to be uneven after sewing. Trim to the pie portion to square up all sides.

Step 5 Sewing the curve. The non-pie piece should be on top because that is the piece that will pucker when it's sewn if you don't keep a close eye on it. I like to see my pleats and puckers coming so I can put the needle down, raise the presser foot, and scoot the extra puckering fabric to the back. Take it slow and you will never have another pucker on your curves!

Step 6 Pressing. In figs. 6a and 6b, you can see how beautifully the seams lie down after pressing. You can press the seam allowance in either direction, but note that if you press the seam allowance away from the pie, the non-pie pops out, and if you press it toward the pie (as in this example), the pie pops out a little.

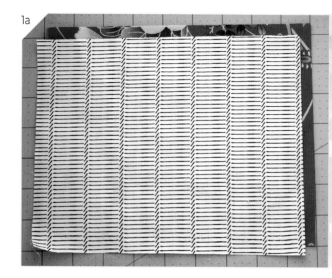

1a

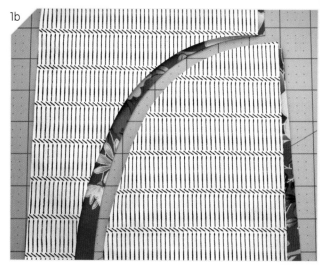

1b

2a

2b

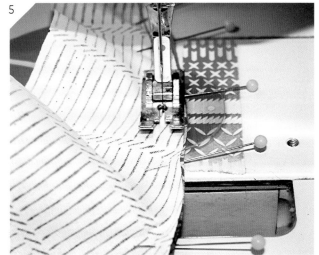

5

3

6a

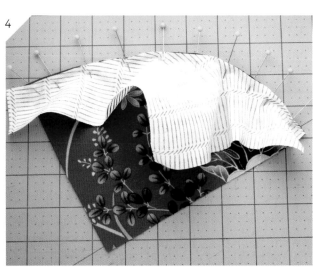

4

6b

Cogs—curves with teeth!

Attach cogs to your curves.

Step 1   First you need to construct your cog strip. This one is only ⁵⁄₈in wide. One of your fabrics needs to be the same as your curve pie piece if you want the cog look. Because the strip is thinner than one inch, I easily curved it with my iron and starch.

Step 2   Pin the cog strip onto the curve, beginning at the curviest part of the curve, and add pins going around the curve from the center toward each end. Remember, the ends won't be even.

Step 3   Sew the cog strip onto the curve and press. The seam will automatically want to be pressed to the curve because of all the seams.

Step 4   Place the curve-cog piece onto a piece of fabric matching the other color of the strip and cut a matching curve.

Step 5   Flip, pin, and sew as usual.

Step 6   Press well. If your outside piece wants to pucker, use water to relax the fabric and it press flat. I usually use starch as well.

TIP: Pin those curves!

4

5

6

CURVES ADDING COGS

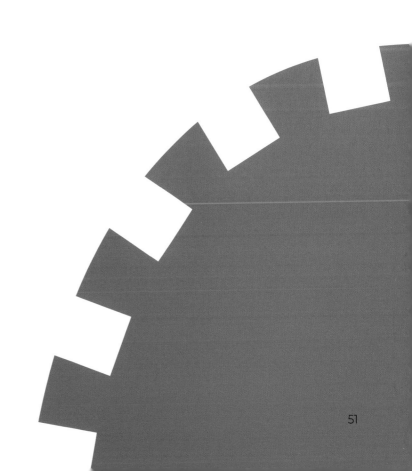

Concentric skinny lines

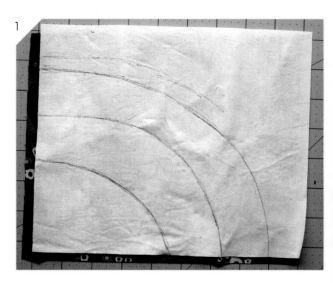

It's fun to alter curves by embedding concentric skinny lines.

Step 1 To start, place two fabrics, face up, on top of each other. Cut the fabrics at least 1½–2in larger than your desired finished size. If you are going to embed more than two or three, you'll want to make the original pieces up to 4in larger because you'll lose size with each embedded line. Remember, you add an $\frac{1}{8}$in skinny line, but lose ½in seam allowance with each line! I sometimes draw my curves onto my fabric for consistency.

Step 2 Start with the smallest curve and cut through both fabrics.

Step 3 Flip, pin, and sew the curve.

Step 4 Press well and place all the fabrics back together to cut the next curve.

Step 5 Repeat steps 3 and 4 until all the lines are cut, pinned, curved, and pressed (figs. 5a and 5b).

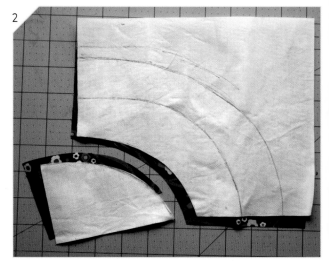

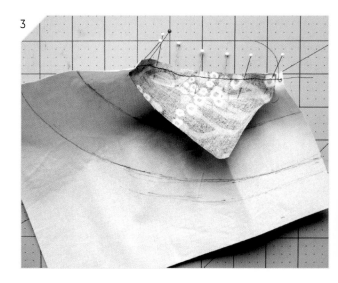

4

5a

5b

CURVES CONCENTRIC SKINNY LINES

Half-circles and embedding strips

Half-circles are done the same way as all curves. The trick is to pin, pin, pin that curve—and take it slowly when you sew.

Step 1   If you want to embed strips into the curved piece, it is best done before cutting the curve in the background fabric (figs. 1a–1c).

Step 2   This is one of the few times that you don't need to cut the curve in both pieces of fabric at the same time. When you are manipulating the curved section by adding strips, the curve can change. It's better to be safe than sorry and wait to cut the background curve when the curved piece is finished.

Step 3   If you do cut them together as usual, after embedding the strips, recut the curves so that they match before sewing them together. The lower edges will not be even. Trim to the straight edge of the curve.

Step 4   Pin and sew.

1a

1b

1c

2

3

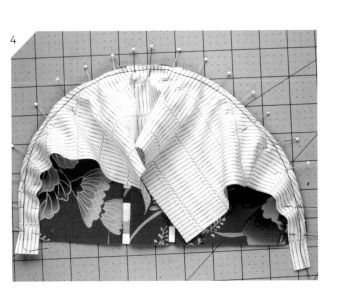

4

CURVES HALF-CIRCLES AND EMBEDDED STRIPS

Skinny lines across curved pieces

There are two methods for sewing skinny lines across curves. You can line up both parts of your curve and slice them together. Sew strips into each section and then sew the curve matching the skinny line, as in figs. 1 and 2.

The other method is to sew the curve first and then embed strips. If you are playing with strip placement, this is the way you want to go. See figs. 3–6.

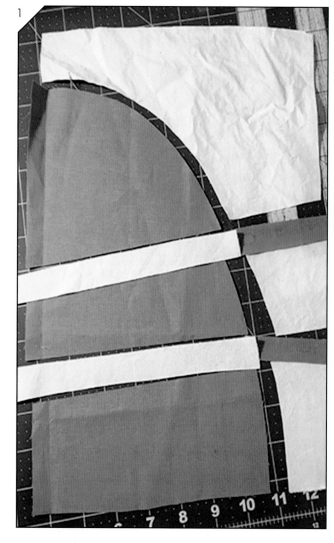

1

2

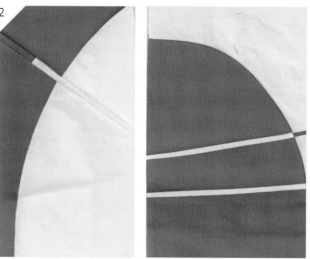

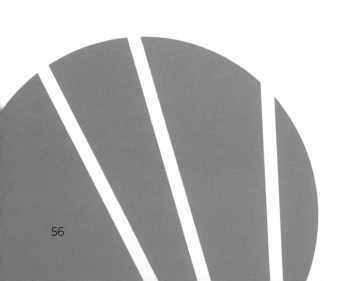

CURVES SKINNY LINES ACROSS CURVED PIECES

3

5

4

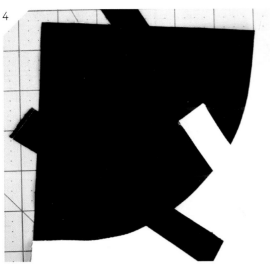

6

Parallel pinning a curve

When slicing across a curve and inserting a strip, the curve will become distorted and jagged unless you make an effort to keep it smooth. The best way to do that is a trick called "parallel pinning." You can see how to do this on the right. Place a pin along where you will sew the seam—¼in from the edge and parallel to the edge (fig. 1). Flip the top piece so you can see how the seam will affect the curve. You may need to fiddle by scooching the fabric back and forth and repinning until it's the curve you want (fig. 2).

1

2

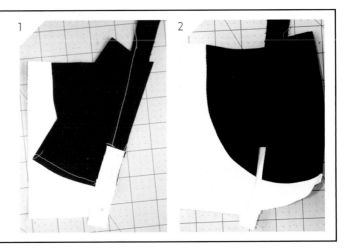

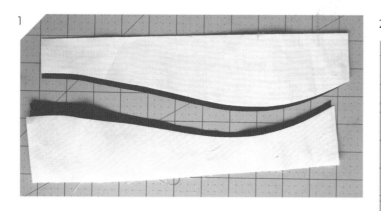

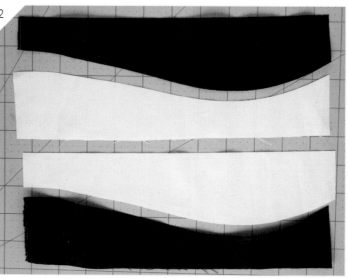

Wave curves

Waves are slow, gentle curves.

Step 1 Begin by placing two rectangles together, right sides up. Cut a gentle curve through both fabrics.

Step 2 Arrange one side of the curve to the opposite color, opposite curve.

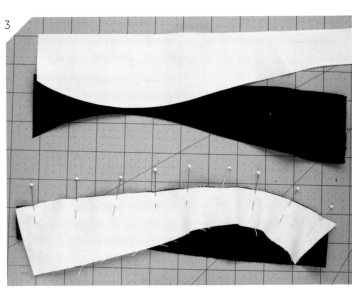

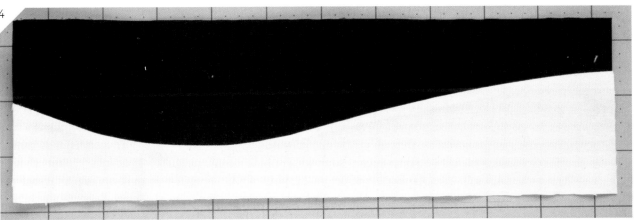

Step 3   Flip one and match the two pieces at the apex of the curve, right sides together. Add pins every inch from the curviest part outward toward the ends and sew.

Step 4   Open and press.

CURVES WAVE CURVES

59

Triangles

Four ways to make three sides

With all their points, triangles add movement. Alone, in a row, or in clusters, they jump and crystallize into interesting patterns. Add half-square triangles (HST), isosceles triangles in myriad positions, or stand-alone mountains or trees to activate your design.

Half-square triangles (HST)

There are ways to make four or eight HST at a time. You can find many tutorials for them online. I do two at a time because I rarely make them all of the same two fabrics and prefer to make just what I want and need.

Step 1 Start by cutting a square $7/8$in larger than the finished size of your triangle.

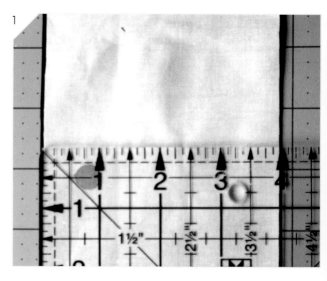

Step 2 Stack two fabrics and cut the square. Draw a diagonal with any writing implement.

Step 3 Sew ¼in on both sides of this diagonal.

Step 4 Cut along the drawn diagonal line.

Step 5 Press seam allowance to dark side and trim to size.

You now have two HST to arrange in many ways to create many different designs: see figs. 6–9 for ideas.

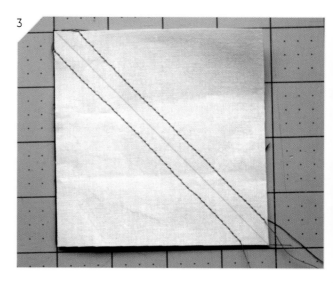

TRIANGLES HALF-SQUARE TRIANGLES

4

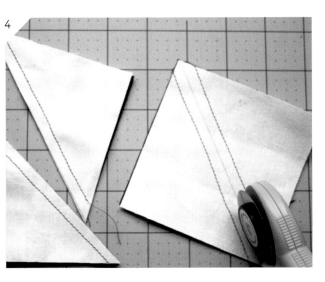

7

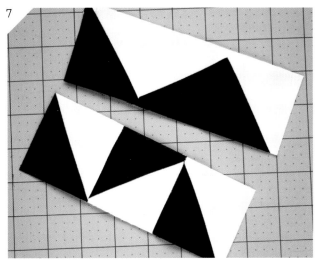

5

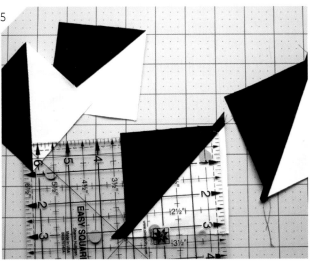

8

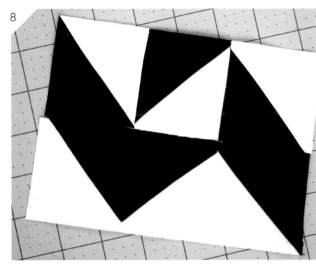

6

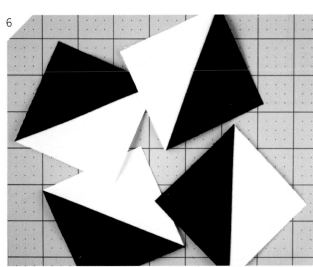

9

Isosceles triangles

An isosceles triangle has two sides of equal length. Whether you make them in only two colors or in many colors, isosceles triangles can be arranged in many ways to make strong patterns. They are fun to play with! They are easy to make, too.

Step 1   Layer four fabrics and cut them into rectangles. The ones I'm using in this photograph are 5in x 4in. Draw a line from the top center point to both lower corners.

Step 2   Divide into colors and flip over the corners, lining up the side edges. Sew with ¼in seam allowancce.

Step 3   Open and press.

Step 4.   Align in whatever pattern you want (figs 4a–4c).

1

2

3

4c

4a

4b

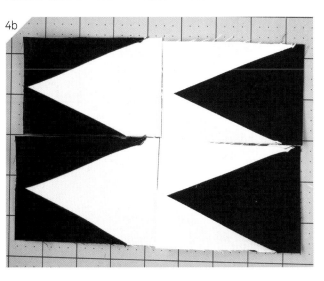

TRIANGLES ISOCELES TRIANGLES

Log cabin triangles

Log cabins can be triangles if you don't need to live in them!

Make them exactly the same way you make square log cabins, except for one thing: in measuring the strip for each round, realize that it needs to be cut to twice the length of the side to which you are attaching it. You are dealing with a diagonal and you need to verify that when opened, you don't lose your points. In figs. 1 and 2, notice that it is simple to use a ruler to determine the length of the strips. The wider the strip you are adding, the longer the strip needs to be.

As with a square log cabin (see fig. 8 on p.47), proceed clockwise until each round is finished (fig. 4). You can also add a stem to make a tree (fig. 5).

TIP: *Never* trim log cabin strips at your sewing machine. Open the seam and press well before you trim to size! You don't want to lose those fine points you just sewed!

TRIANGLES LOG CABIN TRIANGLES

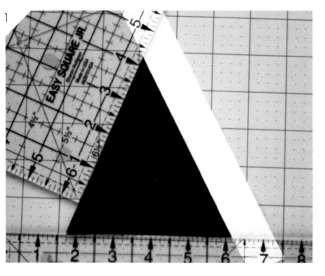

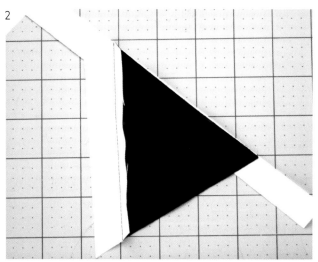

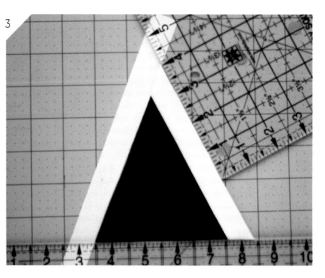

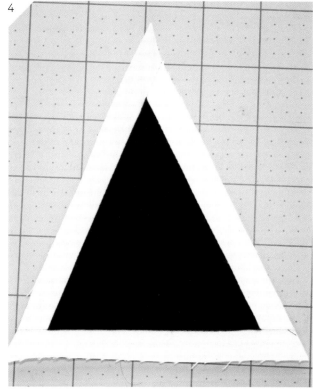

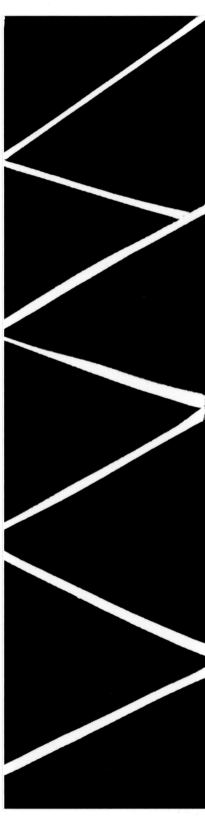

Skinny line triangles

Step 1   To make a row of skinny line triangles, cut a rectangle of fabric 1in wider than you want your finished strip. I cut this one 4in x 14in (10cm x 35.5cm) and the finished dimensions are 3in x 13in (8cm x 33cm). Cut diagonals across the width of the fabric to make triangles.

Step 2   Starting at one end, attach a strip longer than you think you are going to need (that diagonal thing again). Attach the strip with a ¼in seam (figs. 2a and 2b).

Step 3   Repeat Step 2 (figs. 3a and 3b).

Step 4   Press the seam allowance away from the skinny line so that you can see the width of line you are sewing on your next seam.

Step 5   Keep attaching and pressing across the strip until it is as long as you want. I often make it much longer than I need and cut it into sections for extra components.

TIP: For the perfect skinny line, cut the original strip at 3/4in width, sew, trim to $^3/_8$in

---

1
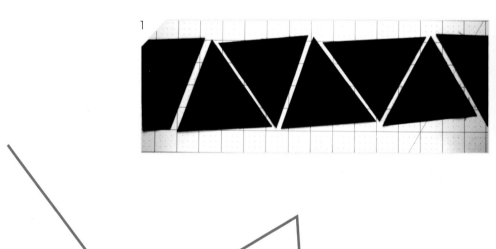

2a

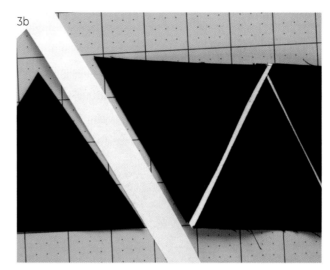

3b

2b

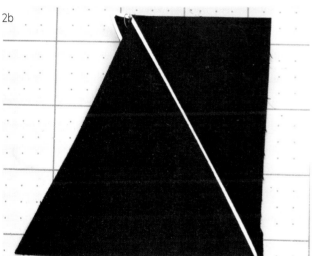

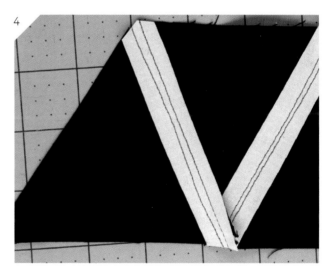

4

3a

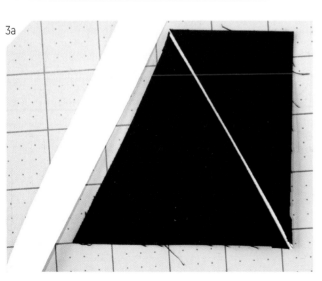

TRIANGLES SKINNY LINE TRIANGLES

Stars

I don't use stars very often in my work, but you may want to include one or two in your piece. Improv stars are most easily made from squares and triangles.

Step 1   Begin the star with nine 3in x 3in squares, eight of the background color and one in the center in the star color.

Step 2   Starting with the top center square, place a rectangle of the star color diagonal across the square. Note that the portion of the square showing will be approximately the size of the star point when sewn.

Step 3   Sew with a ¼in seam.

Step 4   Open and press.

Step 5   Trim loosely to square shape and excess of background on back.

Step 6   Place another rectangle of star fabric diagonally across this square.

Step 7   Sew this up.

Step 8   Trim and square up.

Step 9   Repeat Steps 2–8 on three other background squares and line up to create a star.

Step 10   Sew the squares together in rows.

TIP: *Do not* trim at the sewing machine! *Always* press, then cut to avoid cutting off something wrong!

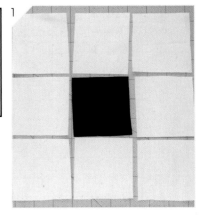

STARS

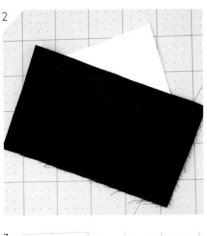

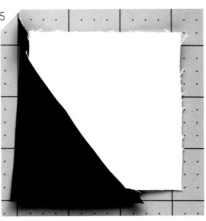

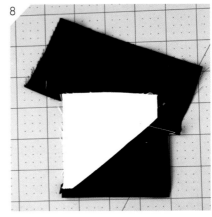

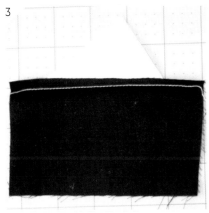

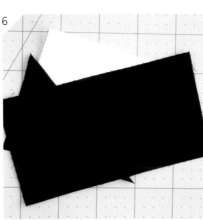

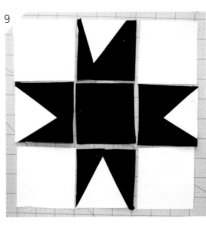

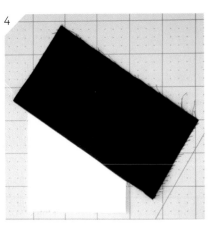

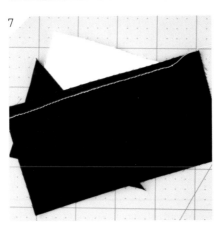

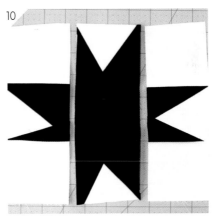

Bits and Slabs

Bits and slabs are components that aren't sewn together into other configurations.

Bits are those little pieces of fabric scattered all over your cutting table, or on the floor, or in your scrap bin. I love to stick little pieces on the wall coming off other components or use longer ones to activate empty spaces.

Slabs are big pieces of fabric in any shape to fill spaces quickly.

Bonnie Raitt started with three large slabs of black. Smaller bits of white, then longer bits of white comprised most of the design.

Markings in Black and Red has many slabs and added bits. Notice the collection of bits that create new components.

Big slabs of black

Markings in Black and Red

Add white bits

BITS AND SLABS

3

Bonnie Raitt

PHASES OF THE PROCESS

There are several stages in making your quilt that seem to occur for everyone in every quilt.

Phase One *I love this!*

The first one is about halfway into the process. I usually love what I am making at that juncture and want to stop because I'm afraid that if I keep going, I am going to ruin it. It is perfect just the way it is. I have to talk myself into continuing. Take a good photo and know that, if indeed you do decide later that you have ruined it, you can always take it back to this stage and either start building in a different direction or finish it.

This is the start of Landscape in Skinny Lines *and I was loving the monochromatic linear quality. I was also intrigued by the asymmetry and geometry. But I wasn't sure I could continue without destroying those qualities.*

Phase Two *I hate this!*

The next stage that always happens is the "I hate it!" stage. This hits at about two-thirds of the way through the design process. You have been looking at it constantly: it has been exciting and all is going very smoothly then—suddenly—you've chosen the wrong colors. It's unbalanced, it's boring, it's too curvy, it's not curvy enough. You want to tear it all off the wall and stomp on it.

Don't. You are just tired. Improv quilting is exhausting. It takes a lot of energy both physically and mentally.

There are two ways forward: I usually forge ahead. I know that with the next few component additions, I will begin to find my way again. I often pick up a scrap off the cutting table and throw it up on the wall. Voila! The design begins to offer new opportunities or opens new spaces. The other option is to let it rest. Go work on something else for a while. I don't suggest starting another improv quilt, I just suggest switching tasks. Work on quilting another piece. Make a charity quilt for your guild. Dye some fabric. When you are ready, begin working anew. Within a few minutes, you will be immersed again and find your way through to liking it again.

Phase Three *I can't believe I made this!*

The most exciting stage is the moment when you step back and the hairs on the back of your neck stand up. Your heart starts beating quickly and you want to jump up and down. This is the moment when you realize that you have tapped into your creativity and something exciting has happened without you even being aware. It happens when the process is working!

Be thoughtful—but don't think!

Phase Four *Help! Should I rearrange this?*

I am now going to contradict everything you've read on the past few pages. I'm going to let you rearrange your design, or tear it down, or add a new color because ...

... sometimes it just doesn't work. It's important to acknowledge that not every attempt will be a masterpiece. My best pieces are always the first of a new series. I can feel the excitement and joy of a new exploration and it transfers into the quilt. I have discovered that the quilts I love most are universally loved most.

I have given up on a few quilts as well. These are the ones that feel derivative or tired. The last piece in a series always looks and feels uninspired. Time to move on to a new exploration.

Sometimes, I give up on the ones that have received comments such as "Looks like two pianos!" "Looks like a big chicken!" Looks like two hawks flying!" I don't want my abstract expressions to be representational. I don't finish those because I can't unsee what has been revealed to me. If it's early in the process, I can change the direction and undo the "image" but if it's almost done, I'll move to a new project.

To determine whether your design is not working or if you are just tired of it and need a break, takes a critical heart-to-heart discussion with yourself. Are you feeling insecure and uncertain? Are you not happy with it because it doesn't look like everyone else's quilts? It's hard to keep going when you haven't had years of art training and think everyone else knows more than you. Step back and try to look at your quilt from a different perspective. Take your ego out of it and look at it as if your best friend were making it. What would you tell her?

Commitment to finish can be difficult. You are welcome to rearrange all your components a million times, but my suggestion is to finish this quilt and start another.

You'll learn something new from every quilt you make, even if it's not your favorite.

Sometimes your piece becomes too precious and you need to explode it! You are really, really happy with what you have made so far, but are "stuck" and don't know where to go next. Many times that is because your composition up to that point has become your only way of looking at it. Take a photo so you can go back there if you want to later and start moving things around. Take everything off the wall, mix it up and rearrange. Find a new color and start inserting it here and there. You need to let the preciousness go in order to get to the other side.

Is it done?

When you feel that your design is complete, study it carefully. Take photos and turn them upside down, 90 degrees clockwise, 90 degrees counter-clockwise. Grab a mirror and look at it in reverse. Look for parts that may need a little something for balance. Maybe there is a section that looks too heavy or too sparse. The quilt will let you know when it is done. If it feels complete to you, it is. It fills the space. It is interesting. It invites your eyes to roam all over the surface and not just jump to one section. It feels balanced. I never start sewing any of my components together until I am happy with my entire design. When I am satisfied that I love it, I take another photograph and print it out as reference for sewing it together.

> **TIP:** Take photos often! Turn them upside down and sideways to get a new perspective on what you are doing.

DESIGNING: A STEP-BY-STEP GUIDE

I created this quilt for this book and I wanted to use all the components (although I couldn't figure out where to put a star!). I knew that the target would be a visually strong element and decided to begin by using it as the keystone, instead of trying to find a place to add it later.

Step 1   I started with the most controversial component—a target! My challenge was to use this statement design element and make it work.

Step 2   I added more log cabin components to "mirror" the center target and also the black and white stripe. By surrounding the center with similar shapes in equally graphic colors, I am incorporating it more into the overall design.

Step 3   I continued adding square elements, but also added a skinny-line log cabin to add more interest and start varying the design.

Step 4   With the center complete, I wanted to head out in other directions. It was time to add a curve. The stripes and checkerboard keep to the graphic feel and activate space to the right and left. So I embedded skinny lines into the curve to balance the skinny-line log cabin.

Step 5   More large curves in black and more skinny lines, but triangles this time. You can see that I'm adding large dark components to add weight to the center. The different shapes and/or direction of each of these creates interest as well. I'm still balancing the black and white stripes across the design to keep the eye bouncing.

Step 6   Moving out. Adding triangles for action in medium sizes. While skinny-line antenna balances skinny line log cabin. Notice how your eye starts to react between the different elements.

1

2

3

4

5

6

DESIGNING A STEP-BY-STEP GUIDE

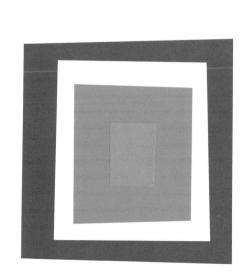

Step 7 Time to add more color. I'm keeping this quilt very graphic by using a lot of black and white, but want to add another color and it's complement for added interest. Notice that I am continuing to work from the center out, and varying scale in some components while also repeating similar elements in others.

Step 8 Continuing to grow. More curves and more skinny lines. I wanted to activate the space to the right and added a lone strip of black. To the left, I threw a couple of little squares and another black strip to move the design toward the edge.

Step 9 More color, more movement. Now I'm trying to balance the color and shapes. The big curve to the far right balances the center and adds a lot of movement.

Step 10 This is an important step. The center is filled and the edges have been activated but I needed to fill the space between these elements. I decided that skinny lines in graceful curves would be perfect, so I added them on both sides. It is important that they are large enough to activate the space, but also that the curves are directional and add more movement.

Step 11 The top left corner is empty and the bottom edge needs more weight, so I added large black objects and dotted/striped components to finish the design.

Notice how completely different the same design appears when made in different colors and fabrics.

See also the step-by-step guide on pages 120–127 to discover exactly how the various components of the quilt come together to make the finished quilt.

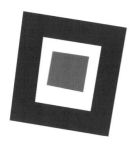

7

8

9

11

10

DESIGNING A STEP-BY-STEP GUIDE

ENGINEERING: SEWING IT TOGETHER

YOUR DESIGN IS NOW DONE!
COMPLETE! FINIS!
IT'S TIME TO SEW IT ALL TOGETHER.

Engineering is the same as piecing—sewing it all together into one single sheet of fabric.

I don't consider how the pieces will be sewn together as I build my quilt. I only focus on the design that I'm making. I always have my entire piece laid out on the design wall before I think about how to put it all together. Even though the design process is my favorite part of improv, the engineering process activates another part of my brain. It's a puzzle to solve and is very rewarding. The appeal of Dancing with the Wall for me is the engagement of each different part of the process. I love that designing uses my creative brain and the engineering joins both sides of my brain: the artsy and the puzzle-solving.

Sewing your components together can look daunting but don't panic! You can do it!

First, take a photograph of your quilt and study it carefully. Identify the longer seams to divide the piece into sections. Draw lines on the photo to help you do this (figs. 1 and 2).

When you have divided the picture of your piece into sections, start construction by sewing small components into larger components. Find adjacent pieces that are similar in size or easily sewn together and sew those first.

As you work, starch and press each seam well. You will find it easier to work with stiffer pieces. Floppy fabric that hasn't been starched stretches more and is harder to control. If you are working with a component with a bias edge, starch extra well and press, don't iron, because it can quickly be ironed out of shape.

This is the time to square off each section as you go. You might need to straighten some components by cutting off diagonal

TIP: Press each and every seam with starch as you work! A floppy fabric doesn't like to behave!

edges or evening up seam edges. Don't worry, this won't affect your overall design.

In some places, you'll need to add more fabric to make a component a little larger and sometimes you might need to trim a piece to fit. I prefer to add fabric to a piece instead of trimming its partner piece. I'd rather have more fabric to work with than perhaps cut something too small. If you do trim, be careful as you do, so as not to affect the component negatively. As an example, if you need to cut down a checkerboard, the trimmed off row will become a row of rectangles instead of squares.

It sometimes helps to use tracing paper to assist in piecing wonky sections. I trace the section while it's on the design wall. Then I take the tracing to the cutting table and place the components on top of it. I find that isolating and laying a section out flat helps with visualizing how to put it together. If you need to add fabric, it's nice to be able to make a pattern from the tracing so that you make the added piece the correct shape and size.

When a section looks very difficult, sketch alternative ways to piece it. This quilt *Flight of the Covid Geese* by Barbara Gillespie is a challenging design to engineer because of the triangles circling the center. These "flying geese" in a circle can be joined in different ways. It's nice to be able to think through them.

What a great job working out a difficult puzzle!

Fig 1. shows how the geese could be sewn into a big circle that can then be divided into smaller sections and attached to the center in arcs.

Fig. 2 shows the way she actually pieced her quilt. She sewed the triangles into longer strips and then joined them with wedges and straight seams.

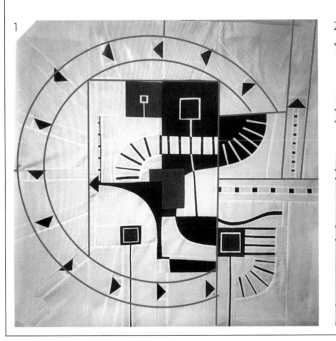

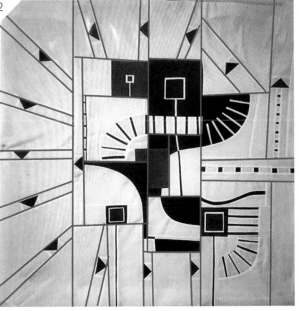

Engineering examples

In the following photographs, I show how I divided a quilt into sections for easier engineering.

To begin, I added background fabric in all the spaces between the components. I measured each space and cut the pieces to fit, making each a couple of inches larger to be safe. I picked out the components that were easy to sew together and made larger components from the smaller ones.

I have broken down three more complex areas (A, B, and C on Fig. 2) to show you how I piece them.

> **TIP:** Everything on the design wall interacts with your quilt design. Keep extra components on a nearby table, not on the wall

ENGINEERING EXAMPLES

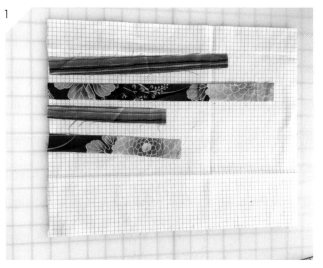

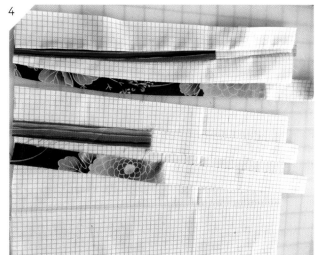

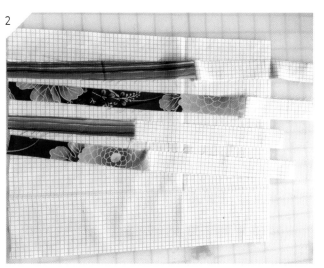

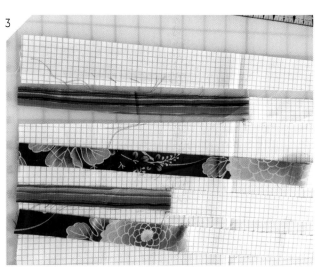

I often have little scraps of fabric stuck on the design wall and need to make them into a component. Or I have several smaller components and need to join them together into the background. I cut a large piece of background fabric and trace the elements onto it. I take it to the cutting table and lay out the components or individual pieces of fabric on top of it. I can then use the fabric directly to cut out each background piece and, working across the section, sew them together in consecutive order, adjusting sizes and shapes as I go. Figs. 1–5.

Notice how I needed to add fabric to make this section fit in the final engineering. I thought carefully about which fabric to add: I could use the red floral background fabric or the turquoise floral. I decided that the white background changed the design too much by separating the pink log cabin and half square triangle sections from the main design. I auditioned the red floral and it was too much red—it threw the composition off balance. Then I auditioned the turquoise, it was just right! When I look at the original design pre-engineering and the completed quilt, it is not noticeable unless you knew I had to alter it.

 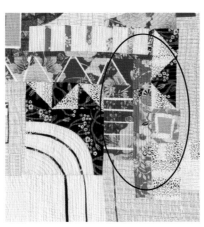

Here is how I engineered the top left corner.

Step 1   Cut a square of the background fabric in the size needed for the corner. Lay out the pieces on top of it where they will be sewn.

Step 2   Cut a strip of the square of background fabric the same height as the striped pieces and sew them together to create a new square. Press well.

Step 3   Place the big corner curve back in place but extend it 1/4in out on the side and top before you cut it.

Step 4   Here is the curve 1/4in out. This extra little bit will allow your curved piece to fit better.

Step 5   Pin and sew the curve. **BUT WAIT!**
It's not laying very smooth! What to do! Luckily there's a way to fix that puffy fabric that is caused by the curve not quite easing in the way it should.

Step 6   Iron the curve flat so that the excess fabric folds into the background fabric. I have drawn a black line where the crease formed. Take it back to the sewing machine and re-sew the curve, sewing on the black line.

MUCH BETTER!

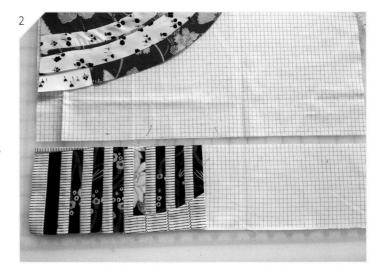

3

6a

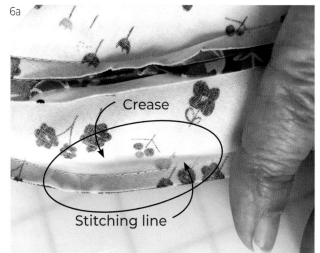

Crease

Stitching line

4

6b

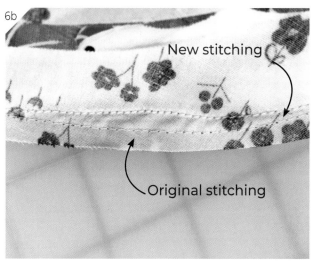

New stitching

Original stitching

5

6c

Engineering challenges

It's difficult to foresee all the ways you will be engineering your quilt.

Here are some of the more common challenges you may face

Partial seams

These are two seams that don't line up. This is how to proceed. But remember: *always sew the longest seam last.*

Step 1 Sew one seam part way.

Step 2 Stop, and fold out.

Step 3 Introduce the other piece of material so that it abuts the partial seam.

Step 4 Sew the other seam

Step 5 Fold out and finish sewing the first seam.

1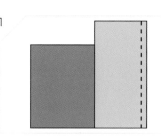

2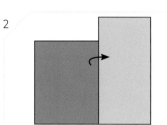

3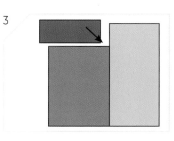

4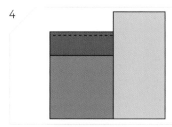

5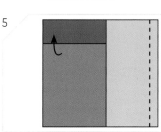

Y-seams

These are actually seams that come together in a Y and are handled differently than partial seams.

Step 1 Position the first piece for sewing.

Step 2 With Y seams, you sew your central seam and stop ¼in short of the top piece of material.

Step 3 Then, sew the second seam and stop a ¼in short of the material

Step 4 With the needle down, turn your piece and line up the other seam. Finish sewing.

1

2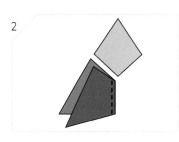

3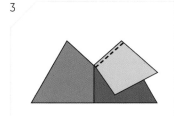

4

5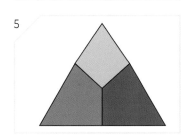

Absolutely impossible

There are some sections that are absolutely, definitely, no-question, impossible to engineer. When you realize you have created these types of sections, you have a couple of options. One choice can be to choose an alternate piecing method, usually appliqué. Another option is to modify your design so that it becomes possible. I have had to modify many sections of quilts and realize that these little tweaks do not make a huge difference in the appearance of my overall quilt.

Appliqué

There are some places where appliqué is the perfect solution to an engineering problem. If you have added smaller decorative elements in your design, the best way to deal with them is by sewing them onto the surface of your finished quilt. In my quilt *Mark Makers Linked*, the large irregular sections became unwieldy when I tried to piece them into the quilt. It dawned on me that the easiest (and therefore the best) way to engineer them would be to leave the large section in the quilt where they belong as a field of white fabric, and appliqué the sections on at the end.

There are various methods of appliqué to consider. In needle-turn appliqué, the pieces are cut ¼in larger on all sides and then the edges are turned under as you sew them on by hand or with a machine.

Raw edge appliqué often uses an adhesive stabilizer applied to the back of the fabric to be appliquéd, this is then ironed in place and overstitched by hand or with a machine.

Adding lines with bias tape strips is another appliqué solution. It is much easier to sew a piece of bias tape on top of a completed quilt top than to try to piece it in.

My quilt, *Balancing Act*, includes both bias tape and raw edge appliqué to construct the design. Alternatively, my quilt *Tattered History of Indigo* is entirely raw edge appliqué. Scraps from various indigo projects were arranged on a large piece of dark blue hand-dyed fabric. I then attached each component

onto the fabric with my sewing machine using a blanket stitch and my zigzag presser foot. This quilt would have been impossible to piece together—even needle-turn appliqué would have been a difficult undertaking. The edges of each piece of raw edge appliqué frays, and I loved the ragged feeling it provided on the surface of this quilt.

Paper piecing

Paper piecing is a piecing technique in which paper is used as a foundation to make a component. I don't use it in my improv quilts, but it could be handy if you know you want to make a complex component. Making a wonky star would perhaps be easier with paper piecing than trying to construct one from scratch. *Partners In Shine*, a mini-quilt I made for a "Curated Quilts" mini-quilt challenge, ended up being paper pieced. I was frustrated and discouraged with trying various ways to piece the stars. I drew a star on paper and then cut a pattern for paper piecing (I am nothing if not stubborn). There are many tutorials online with instructions for paper piecing. I don't know enough to show you how.

The more you do it, the easier it is!

BUILDING A SMALL QUILT STEP-BY-STEP

Step 1   All laid out with elements placed.

Step 2   I'll complete the semicircle section first. I begin by drawing chalk lines on both sides of the antenna piece.

Step 3   Chalk lines in place.

Step 4   Slice through fabric ½in inside the chalk lines. I will be sewing the antenna sections here.

> **Tip:** Your quilt will shrink as you engineer it because of seam allowances—you might have to rethink some sections.
> It's just part of the process and won't change the final "look" of your quilt

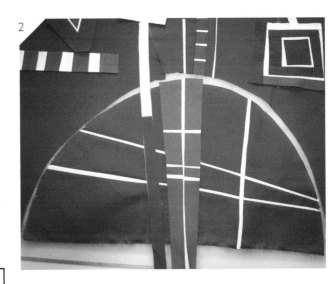

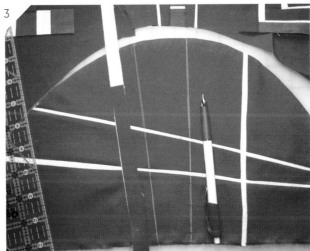

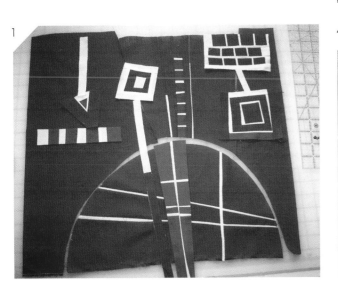

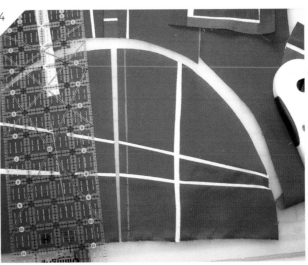

Step 5 Sew antenna section to right side. Press well. Please notice that the chalk line to the left is visible because I cut inside it.

Step 6 Now that antenna is embedded, cut a single slice through the semicircle where the red/white line will go.

Step 7 Sew in the red/white line. Trim the semicircle back to a smooth curve.

Step 8 The semicircle section is now complete. Time to tackle the top right corner section.

Step 9 The top right elements are not the same widths. I need to add red to both sides of them to make them all match for easier construction.

Step 10 Red extensions are added.

Step 11 Sew the elements together and trim.

Step 12 I had to unpick the element to the left in order to embed the top right section.

Step 13 Place squared off elements on top of the right-side piece and cut the piece adding ½in seam allowance.

Tackle difficult things first thing in the morning. When you're fresh, but still a bit foggy

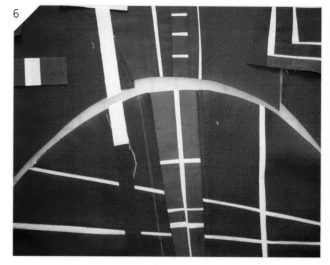

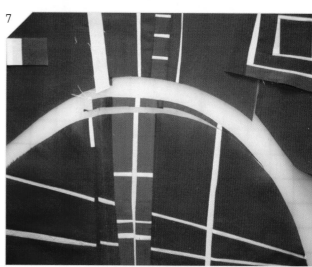

BUILDING A SMALL QUILT STEP-BY-STEP

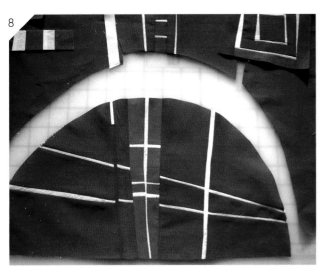

8

11

9

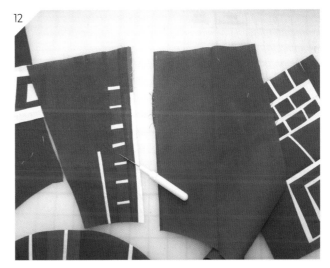

12

10

13

Step 14 Before sewing squared off element to the lower section, check that the two sections will line up after they are sewn together.

Step 15 On to the top left section: once again, I need to unpick the center element from the left side.

Step 16 To create a stem for the log cabin, slice through the left top side and sew in a red and white combination strip.

Step 17 The easiest way to embed the log cabin is to cut through the red background piece. I added red to both sides of the log cabin to make it as wide as the background

Step 18 Embed the log cabin by cutting across the background piece ½in higher than you want the log cabin to sit. Sew the seam. Press. Slice through the background ½in lower than the top of the log cabin, and sew.

Step 19 The semicircle, the top right section, the center section, and the log cabin sections are now done.

Step 20 Now for the top-left section. Add red to both sides of the white stem and to the triangle to square them off. Slice through and insert. Insert the dotted line.

Step 21 Sew all the top pieces together, press, and trim.

Step 22 Now white needs to be added to the top of the semicircle to create the dividing line. Place it on top of the white fabric and cut the curve. Sew.

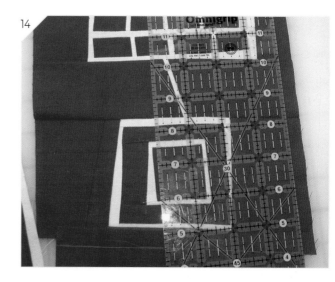

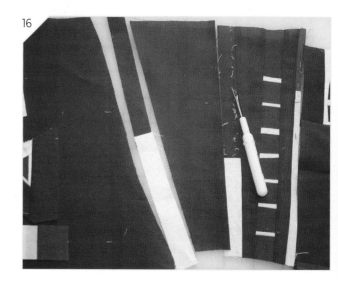

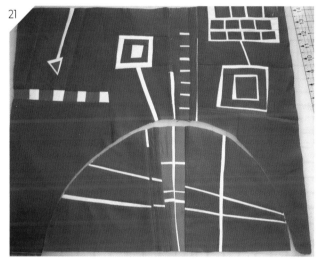

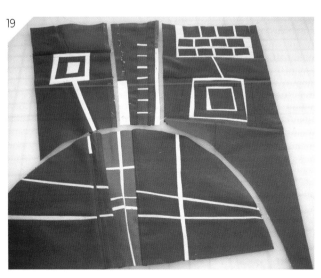

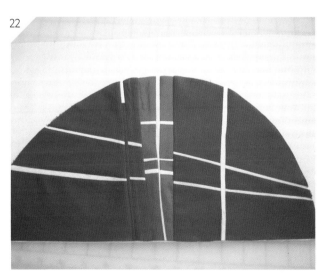

BUILDING A SMALL QUILT STEP-BY-STEP

Step 23 Lay the top piece on top of the white fabric and draw the line where the seam will be sewn with a fabric marker.

Step 24 The line has been drawn. Cut ¼in outside of the line for the seam allowance then sew and press.

DONE!

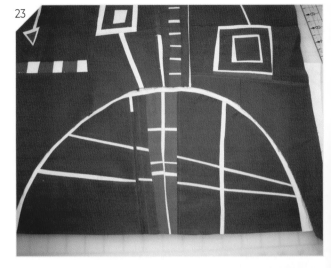

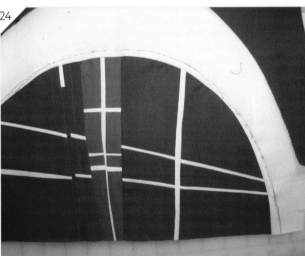

Note: if you compare the finished piece (b) with (a) of the piece prior to construction, there are subtle differences. The white stem of the log cabin no longer lines up. The stems are narrower for all the sections. The curve of the semicircle is not as steep. None of these changes bother me. I think the piece still reads as the same design, but is not quite as wonky.

When you engineer your quilt, there will necessarily be changes because of added fabric or seam allowances. Some lines will be thinner: some shapes won't be the exact same angle. This is the nature of the process and shouldn't concern you. All-in-all, the piece is similar enough—and is all sewn into a single piece of fabric.

BUILDING A SMALL QUILT STEP-BY-STEP

a

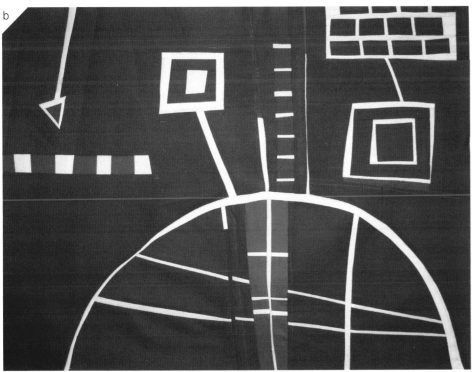

b

93

QUILTING: MAKING IT INTO A QUILT
It's all together! Now let's quilt it!

Yay! You've finished your quilt top and can move on to the next step: the quilting itself. You are probably thinking that your decision-making days are over—not so fast! There are more things to consider that will have an impact on your quilt. You need a backing. You need batting. You need to finish the edges. You need to attach a label.

I love the quiet and calm of quilting and binding. It is during these less exciting, more monotonous tasks that my brain is percolating and the next quilt is beginning to take form in my imagination.

A quilt is a "sandwich" made from the pieced top—also called a flimsy—a layer of batting in the center, and a fabric backing joined together with "quilting." Go figure.

There are thousands of ways to quilt a quilt. You can quilt it on a standing long-arm machine or a sitting long-arm machine. You can quilt it on your domestic sewing machine. You can hand quilt it. You can tack-tie it with thread or yarn. I suggest you look at all the kinds of quilting and see what appeals to you most but also, more importantly, to which method you have access.

Big machines are very expensive, but many fabric stores have in-house long-arm machines that you may rent by the day, or hour, and can include instruction. Quilting on your domestic machine is handy but can be challenging. Almost all sewing machines today come with a free-motion darning foot and a walking foot. The free-motion foot creates a looser, freer type of quilting, while the walking foot is great for straight lines or large curves. Hand quilting is beautiful, but enormously time-consuming—but if you have the inclination, go ahead!

Double Wedding Ring (detail)

Left: Shell Game (detail)

Mary Hogan Block Party

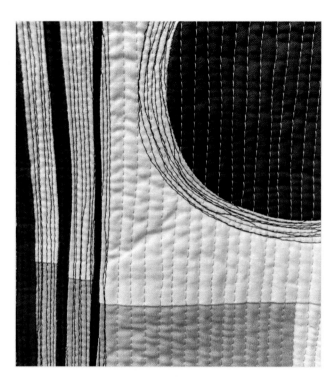

Presenting the Illusions of Calm *by Donna Blalock*

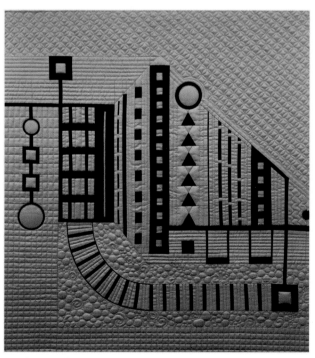

Dusk 2020 *by Marilyn Knepp*

All Those Little Men *by Amanda Ruden*

Backing

The backing is the large piece of fabric that will be the literal back of your quilt. This can be one huge piece of fabric, a couple of pieces sewn together, or in some instances, another opportunity to use pieced blocks or components. Many quilters spend as much time on their quilt backs as they do on the fronts, making it another interesting element in the quilt. I know a quilter who makes some of her quilts double-sided. They are magnificent! They are two quilts in one.

I normally use 108in (274cm) fabric that I get when it's on sale. Once I'm done with the front, I don't worry much about the back. This is probably from my painting background because paintings don't have backs! I also am aware that most of my quilts will be hung on the wall, not thrown on a bed. I wish more of my quilts would end up on beds, but let's be honest, they don't. I use the wide backing in a single fabric because I don't want extra seams to "feel" when I'm working on my sit-down quilting machine. I use my sensitive fingertips to ferret out puckers forming on the underside of my quilt while I am quilting it and seams can confuse the issue.

I'm also unlikely to have many extra blocks or pieces of fabric to use on the back of a quilt. If I have extra components, they normally will be the beginning of another quilt.

I suggest using good quality cotton fabric or for extra comfort, cotton flannel for your backings. I find that it stays smoother and flatter during quilting and is a more pleasurable tactile choice than cheap, stiff, coarse fabric.

Batting

Batting, also called wadding, is the filling in your quilt sandwich. It is the layer that determines how fluffy and warm your quilt is or isn't. It determines the look of your quilt as well. A thin batting will not show the texture of quilting as much as a high loft (loft = thickness).

There are many different types of batting to consider for your quilt. It's important to think about what it is made out of and the loft. Battings are made of cotton, wool, bamboo, polyester, silk, and even "green" batting made from recycled plastic bottles—and combinations of these materials. Each material has distinctive characteristics. I suggest you try out different types until you find your favorite. I'm currently using 80/20 cotton/wool batting because I like the drape and weight.

Battings come in different lofts or thicknesses. For a smoother look, choose a low loft batting $\frac{1}{8}$– $\frac{1}{4}$in loft. For a fluffy quilt, choose a higher loft. The highest is 1in thick and will allow you to make a quilt with a more 3D effect. You also want to consider how you are going to quilt your piece when choosing a batting. Thinner battings are easier to use on a domestic or sitting long-arm machine because of the reduced bulk and weight when you are wrestling your quilt. A long-arm quilting machine, however, can handle any type of batting without problems.

Some battings also have adhesive on one side so that you can iron them to your backing. I find this helpful for keeping all three layers pucker-free, but I don't really like the feel of this batting. I prefer to use a spray or sprinkle-on adhesive with a regular batting. Be careful to follow directions and only use in a well-ventilated space or outside—it's a little scary to think of inhaling the adhesive.

My quilts often have white backgrounds. Some battings are bleached and are much whiter than unbleached. I also found some battings have black dot-things in them and I don't want to use anything that will dull my colors or yellow my whites.

If a quilt is going to be used a lot and therefore thrown in a washer a lot, a poly-cotton batting holds up well. Wool holds water and takes much longer to dry. If you are making a baby quilt, choose a thin cotton batting. You don't know if the baby will have allergy issues, besides it might make a baby too warm.

If you are making a wall-hanging and not highlighting the quilting, a white flannel is a nice replacement for a thicker batting. It is also the preferred inner layer for wearables. Be aware that flannel needs to be pre-shrunk. It has a horrible reputation of shrinking up to 2in and can destroy the finished shape of that beautiful jacket or quilt!

Wool is the lightest batting and is used a lot in warmer climes. It is cooler and lighter than the others. Battings containing polyester are the warmest because they don't breathe as well as natural fibers.

Batting can be purchased by the roll, by the yard, and by pre-determined sizes. These sizes are craft, crib, single, double, queen, and king sizes to match bed sizes. When purchasing pre-packaged batting, the packaging will have the size in inches and the loft on the label.

Thread

I never gave thread much thought when I started quilting. I just used white polyester or the cotton thread I had in my old sewing box. Then I bought my Bernina Q20 quilting machine. The old wooden spools were not appropriate for this beauty. I needed the fancy big standy-up spools I saw in the quilting store. But what kind? Research ensued.

I know now there are many, many, kinds and brands of thread available for piecing and quilting our projects. Thread weights range from teensy tiny 100-weight (the higher the number, the thinner the thread) to size 8 embroidery threads and even thicker. They come in many materials: silk, cotton, polyester, nylon, Kevlar. And types: invisible, water-soluble, metallic, glow-in-the-dark, and on spools, and cones, and bobbins. They come in every color of the rainbow, some are neon, some clear, some variegated. Each of these threads creates different effects. You can quilt with any of them and it is great fun to play with the different looks they will contribute to your work.

I now use the threads that my machines prefer. My quilting machine likes a 40-weight polyester on top and a 50-60 weight poly or cotton bobbin. Anything thinner in the top shreds while I'm stitching long lines. My domestic machine

is an old Singer and only likes the original spools I had in my sewing box. It loves 40-weight cotton in both the top and bobbin. I also have a Bernina 930 that is quite fond of 40-weight top and 50-weight bobbin.

I have also discovered variegated threads, and I love them for special quilts that need a touch of interest and color. I even tested every brand of black and white variegated for my dark quilts in order to find the right repeat length for what I was doing. I've also used them on my hand-dyed brightly colored quilts. They are very fun to quilt with because they keep your eyes jumping as they change color!

There are many specialty threads in weights appropriate for hand quilting, especially big stitch quilting. Embroidery threads in a 12- or 8-weight are beautiful and come in every color. When machine quilting use a 30-weight thread in a contrasting color if you want your quilting stitches to stand out. If you want your stitching to play a lesser role, choose a thinner thread such as a 40- or 50-weight in a color that matches your fabric colors.

If you are needle-turn appliquéing, 80- or 100-weight silks and polyesters make lovely invisible stitches. Personally, I find that threads that are too thin just slip through my fingers and out of my needle while I'm sewing. I now hand appliqué with a 60-weight polyester thread.

Some thread companies helpfully print the size needle to use with their threads on the labels, others have charts on their websites. It's important to use the correct needle for the weight of the thread and the project you are working on. If you are having trouble with thread breaking or skipped stitches while machine quilting, do some research on the website for your thread company, and change your needle to the recommended size and style.

QUILTING THREAD

1, 13	Madiera poly 40 wt
2	Coats All Purpose poly 40 wt.
3, 4, 16, 17	DMC Cotton Embroidery
5	Guttermann poly 40 wt
6	Aurifil cotton 50 wt
7	Guttermann Invisible Thread,
8	Invisible Thread, brand unknown
9	Glide poly 40 wt
10	Aurifil Cotton 40 wt
11, 15	Sulky Rayon 40 wt
12	Isacord
14	DMC cotton embroidery floss

FINISHING
Binding

Binding is the last step in your design process. Whew! Almost done! What an accomplishment! Although you may not see the binding as an element that needs much attention, it is as important a decision as all the others you have made. The edges of the quilt need to be finished off neatly and securely.

You can use a binding that is a strip of fabric that wraps around the front and back edges, or a "facing" that wraps completely to the back for a clean, contemporary look. There are many ways to sew bindings and facings and most quilters will have their favorite methods. You can find instructions in books and on the Internet.

In my work, I use either a single-color binding, a multicolor binding, or a facing.

A single color binding creates a "frame" around the edge of a quilt and gives it a nice, neat, finish. There are numerous tutorials on how to make bindings for quilts.

A fussy cut binding is made using different colors in the binding to accent and enhance the design in your quilt.

A facing wraps around to the back of the quilt leaving your quilt frame-free and gives a contemporary, clean finish.

Exercise your creativity and grow your skills

Above; Austin Skyline

Right: Covid Spring

Above: Balance

Labeling

Label your quilt! You have just spent an inordinate number of hours making your quilt and probably an immense amount of money on all your supplies, machines, and fabrics. Your quilt will last for hundreds of years and be passed down to your relatives. Take credit for your amazing work and let future generations know your name, when you lived, where you lived, and the specific date on which you made the quilt. You can include your website, email address, or Instagram handle on your label as well. Just think how fun that they will appear quaint in a hundred years!

If I am making a casual quilt to throw over my feet in winter, I might write my information on the backing or along the back of my binding in fabric pen. For a formal quilt, I have designed and printed labels from a fabric printing company. There are companies that make generic labels that you can purchase and fill in your information with a fabric pen. It's important to use a fabric pen that is acid-free and permanent.

And that's it!

Your masterpiece is complete.

All that remains is putting it out there into the world for all of us to enjoy. It may be a gift. It may be intended as an entry into an exhibition. It may be for your personal use. Whatever your intention, let others enjoy it as well. Show it to your guild. Post it on Facebook and Instagram. Revel in your accomplishments and be proud of what you've made.

IRENE RODERICK DESIGN

hixsonir@utexas.edu   ireneroderick.com

Let it go! Let it flow! Don't force it!

HOW I DANCE!

MY DANCING STEPS

Over the next few pages, I show you the progression of some of my quilts. My quilts tend to have a "heart" and then become figurative against a light background. For each quilt, I start in the center of my design wall and build out. You will notice that not only do I use the components I've shown you in the book, but also frequently use larger slabs of fabric and the tiny strips found on my cutting table.

The diagrams show how I let the quilt grow organically in all directions throughout the entire design process. The sections in the diagram that are lighter show the earlier steps, while the darker sections indicate the new components I've added in that step.

How will your progression look?

CLINGING TO THE EDGE

SHE'S LOST CONTROL AGAIN

MR. BOJANGLES, DANCE

DRAWING IN BLACK AND WHITE

MARKINGS IN BLACK AND RED

FOGGY DAYS

JOHN PRINE

Clinging to the Edge
56 x 72in
2018

1

3

2

4

HOW I DANCE!

She's Lost Control Again
48 x 65in
2019

1

3

2

4

HOW I DANCE!

Mr. Bojangles, Dance
60 x 76in
2018

1

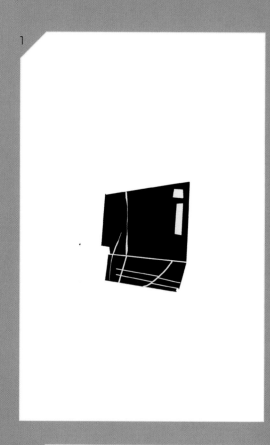

3

2

4

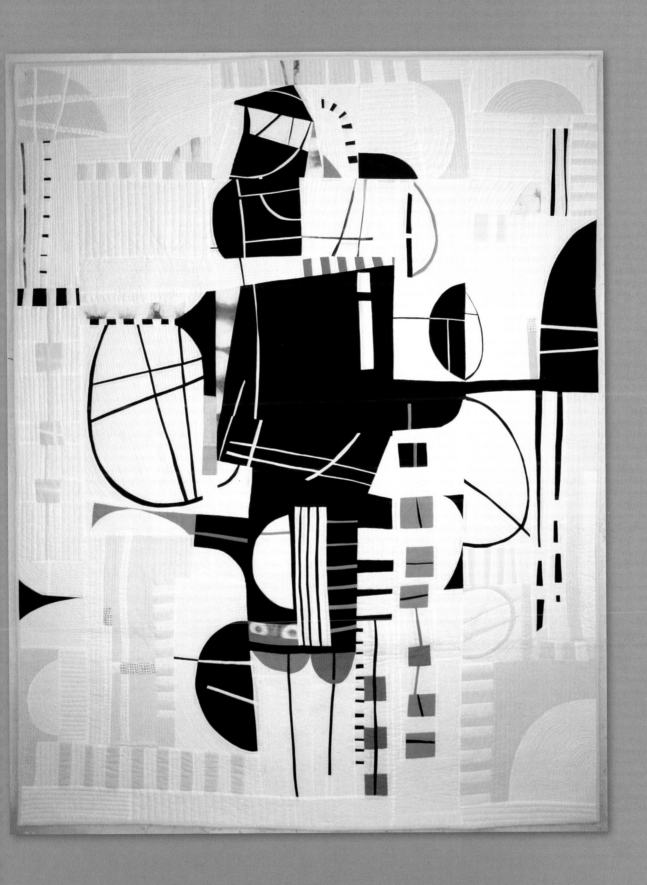

HOW I DANCE!

Drawing in Black and
White
57 x 71in
2019

1

3

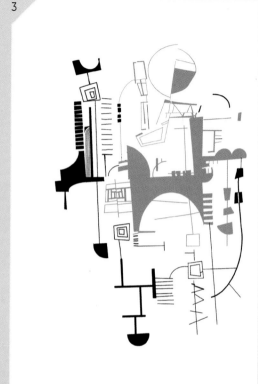

2

4

HOW I DANCE!

Markings in Black and Red
52 x 62in
2020

1

3

2

4

Foggy Days
63 x 78in
2020

1

3

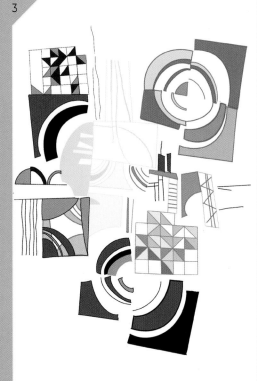

2

4

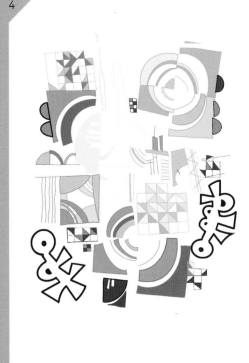

John Prine
55 x 63in
2020

1

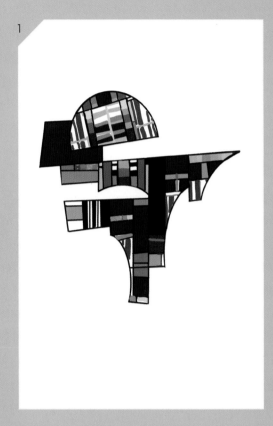

3

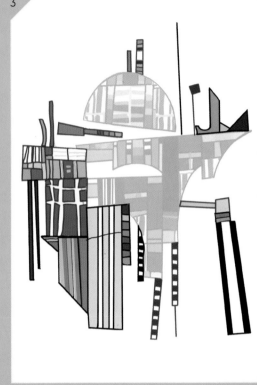

2

4

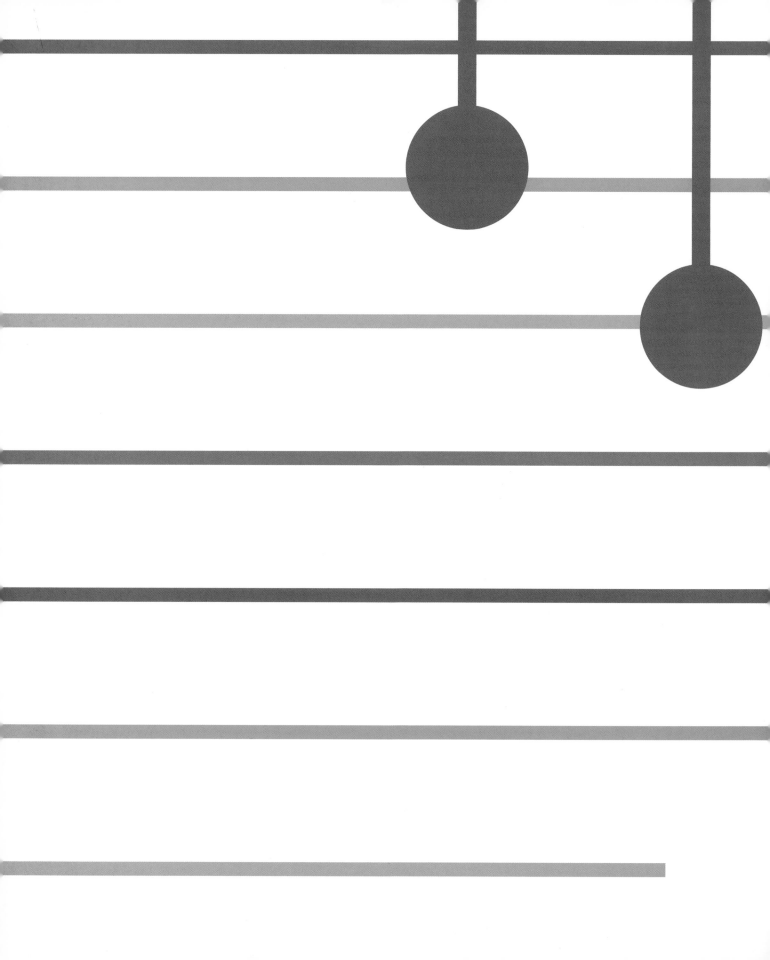

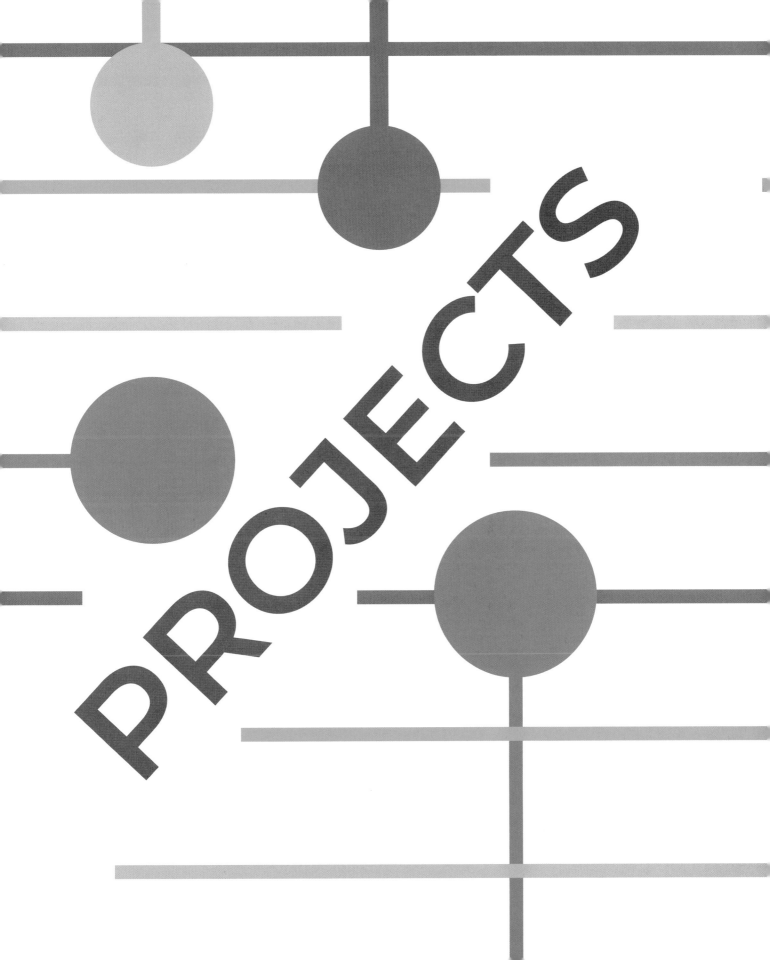

PROJECTS

THE PROJECT QUILTS

A FULL-SIZE QUILT

I designed this quilt as a sampler of the components I explained earlier. Every component (except the star) has found its way into my design. The finished quilt is about 50in x 60in (127cm x 152cm).

So that you can make one similar to it, I have provided a page of thumbnails showing where each component goes, and the page it's on in the book. I have also provided a chart of the sizes that the unfinished components will measure prior to construction. You don't need to follow the instructions at all if you don't want to—you can substitute other components. You can make them different sizes. Go crazy!

You'll notice that there are lots of background areas to fill with fabric after you've put your components in place. Measure and cut those out of the background fabric and place them where they will go before you start putting it together.

You can play with your favorite colors on the coloring page I have included on page 124. What about making the background dark and the components light? What about adding more color and making the entire design bright and cheerful!

I have made this quilt with florals that I have on my bed! While I was making it, I took photographs of how I divided it into sections to more easily engineer it.

Please note that this quilt is under construction so that you may more easily see the separate components prior to assembly.

Ode to Calder

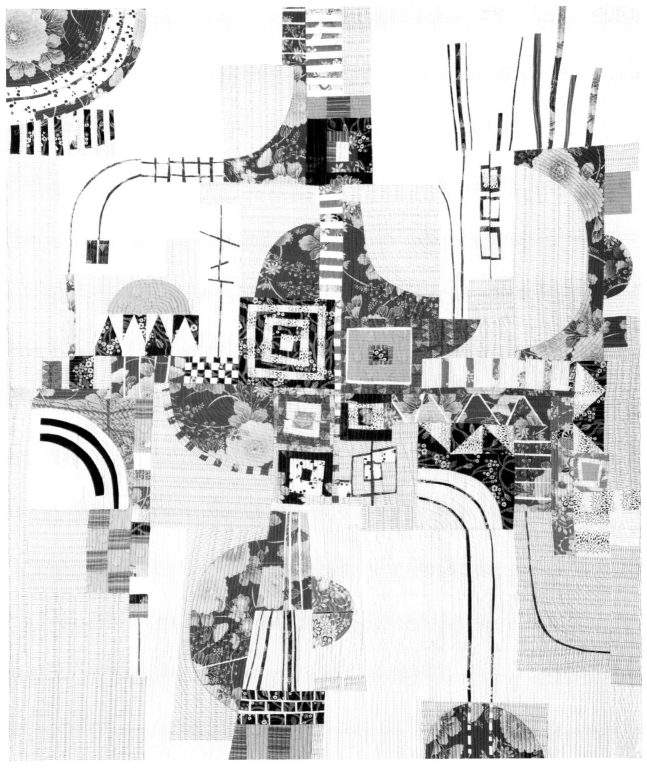

THE PROJECT QUILTS

Spring Garden

Coloring Page

THE PROJECT QUILTS

What if you make the quilt in all blues?

How fun is this quilt in bright and cheerful colors!

1

Maybe you want to try out the components on something a little smaller. I took parts of the quilt and tucked them into two 24in x 24in (61cm x 61cm) mini quilts. I made mine into big fat pillows to throw on my comfy chair.

THE PROJECT QUILTS

2

Each component corresponds to the isolated images on page 122 for easier identification.

Component	Finished size
35	8.75in x 10in
58	4.5in x 4.25in
48	25in x 7in
41	2.5in x 7in
19	3.5in x 7in
51	2in x 8.75in
7	4.25in x 4.25in
8	4.25in x 4.25in
5	2in x 8.5in
42	8in x 7in
37	9in x 7.5in
28	4in x 9in
9	7in x 6.5in
42	8in x 7in
10	3in x 13in

BLACK AND WHITE MINI

I love this mini as a graphic pillow!

Follow the diagram of components in the sizes below for a final project size of 24in x 24in (61cm x 61cm).

Please note: there are four sections that you will need to fill in with white or a component of your choice.

THE PROJECT QUILTS

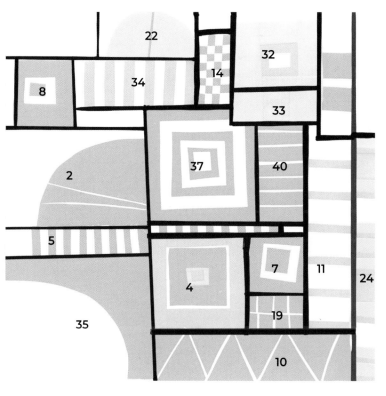

Each component corresponds to the isolated images on page 122 for easier identification.

COLOR MINI

This mini can be a companion pillow to the *Black and White Mini* or standalone. Use any colors or prints that you want to make it completely your own.

Follow the diagram below for a 24in x 24in (61cm x 61cm) finish.

There are empty spaces in this quilt that can be filled in with white or any component you want.

Component	Finished size
35	8.75in x 10in
22	4.5in x 4.25in
34	25in x 7in
32	2.5in x 7in
33	3.5in x 7in
14	2in x 8.75in
7	4.25in x 4.25in
8	4.25in x 4.25in
5	2in x 8.5in
40	8in x 7in
2	9in x 7.5in
4	4in x 9in
19	7in x 6.5in
11	8in x 7in

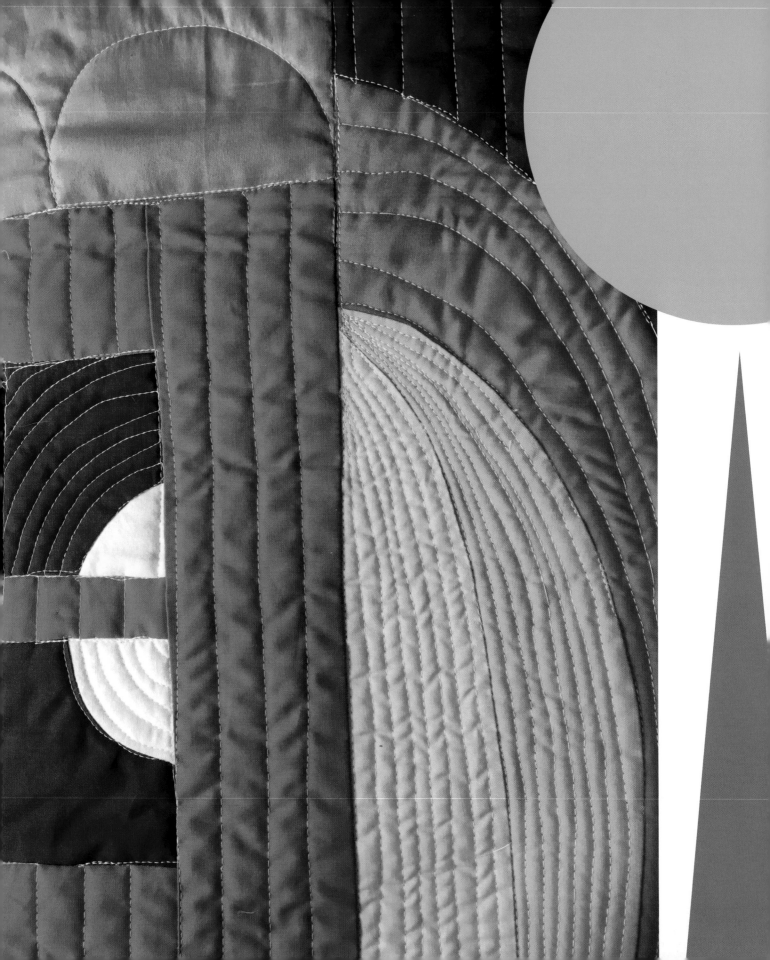

IRENE'S
QUILTS

IRENE'S QUILTS

I began my quilting career in 2016 after retiring from a full-time administrative position in the Department of Art and Art History at a local university. During 2015, I had started dabbling with quilting by taking classes and making small projects, but it wasn't until 2016 that I started quilting seriously when I took a deep-dive into the medium by designing and constructing my own original quilts.

The following pages show a selection of my quilts in chronological order. You will see how various influences appear in my work as I learned how to quilt, improved my skill level, and developed a personal practice.

My early pieces experimented with the aesthetic of "modern" quilts. I designed these on graph paper based on the striking quilts I had seen at QuiltCon 2015. It was important to me to capture a clear, simple design in solid fabric colors. My first successful attempt was *Primarily Minions*. I started the design by playing with the shapes and colors of the Minions in the children's movie *Despicable Me* that my grandson and I loved watching together!

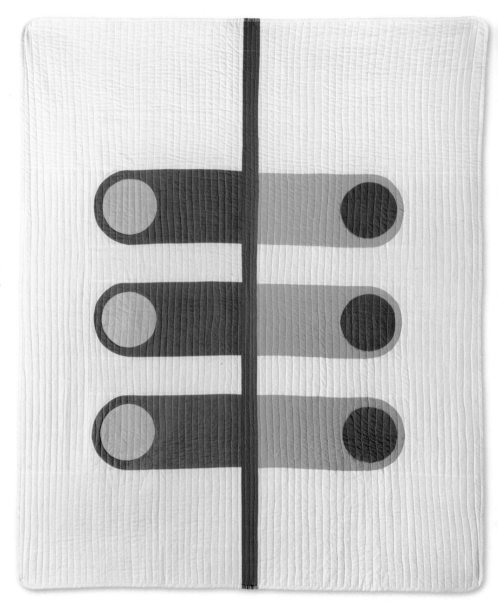

Primarily Minions

Green Magnetism

I was excited by circles, and they grew to fill entire spaces in *Green Magnetism*. At that time I was also making a Double Wedding Ring quilt as a wedding gift for my son, Taylor. I played with the design and the circles, ending up with *Send In the Clowns*.

IRENE'S QUILTS

Send In the Clowns

Another major influence on my work was an obscure Austrian printmaker. One day while on a road trip with friends, our conversation turned to a discussion of favorite artists. My friends started talking about how much they liked the works of an eccentric artist called Friedensreich Hundertwasser. I had never heard of him but was intrigued by their descriptions of his use of brilliant colors and complex designs. I purchased a book on his work and soon after, stuck without an idea for my next quilt, started studying his prints. I noticed that many of his design elements looked like the traditional log

Oompa Loompa Lake House

cabin quilt block. I started making log cabins in bright colors and placed them on my design wall in various configurations. As the piece grew, I began adding strips and squares of solid fabrics emulating his use of color. The resulting quilt, *Oompa Loompa Lake House*, and the next, *Crazy Town Roopetoope*, and the many others that followed are based on his gestures, shapes, and colors. The discovery of his paintings, prints, and architectural projects fundamentally changed how I quilted, and was a first step toward my improvisational quilts that were to follow.

IRENE'S QUILTS

Crazy Town Roopetoope

I was becoming more comfortable with sewing together odd shapes and throwing fabric on the wall in fun, interesting, patterns. I noticed my designs loosening up and becoming more playful. I was no longer thinking or obsessing about making "quilts," as much as experimenting and pushing myself to see what I could make.

I loved challenging myself to see what I could sew together successfully—and what just wasn't physically possible. These quilts were no longer similar to Hundertwasser's work but becoming a unique creative expression of my own. *Gone But Not Forgotten* was a homage to my two sisters who have passed away, and *Balancing Act* are good examples of this period.

Gone But Not Forgotten

IRENE'S QUILTS

Balancing Act

Enter Indigo. A good friend introduced me to natural dyes by asking if I was interested in making an indigo vat. I had no clue what she meant, but it sounded fun. She had worked with indigo dyeing but did not have the space for a vat at her home. We made an organic henna indigo vat and I kept it in my kitchen. I learned about the daily care and attention the vat required and watched over it. Over the next year we investigated the many ways fabric could be dyed. We started a weekly group that we named "Indigo Damen," because "Indigo Girls" was already taken and "Indigo Ladies" sounded too formal. Together, we learned how to *shibori* (Japanese resist dyeing technique) and *sashiko* (Japanese stitching technique) from books and websites. We dyed countless yards of fabric in beautiful blues with an amazing array of patterns.

Wanting to increase our palette, we ordered other natural dyes such as fustic, madder, cochineal, and logwood. We saved avocado pits and onionskins and dyed with them. We also started playing with fiber-reactive dyes because we were interested in brighter colors than we could get with

My Four Sons

Tattered History of Indigo

IRENE'S QUILTS

natural dyes. Because we were getting all of our information from books and through experimentation, I think we developed a much stronger knowledge than we would have if we had just taken workshops in dyeing. There's nothing like getting your hands dirty (literally!) to really understand a process.

The indigo quilts shown here are *My Four Sons*, *Tattered History of Indigo*, and *Happy Hair, Skinny Legs*.

Happy Hair, Skinny Legs

My quilt practice was continuing to evolve. As I developed my skills, my quilts were becoming more complex and sophisticated. I was beginning to challenge myself in design as well. I wanted to investigate how to create visual movement in a quilt using only piecing methods.

Through all this I was determined to keep my quilts as functional, utilitarian objects. I have painted for forty years and couldn't see a need for me to make any more pieces to hang on a wall.

I've always loved the idea of art being functional and functional items being art. I have built and painted furniture, and designed needlepoint projects. I have painted umbrellas, and shoes, and walls. This new medium I had discovered captured the scale and methodology of making my paintings, but could also be used to keep my feet warm!

Looking For Vision

IRENE'S QUILTS

Because my quilts were so different, I was often asked by fellow quilters if I could develop a class to show them how to make crazy improv quilts like mine. But I had no idea how to develop a workshop on my quilting methods: my process is improvisational, not based on patterns, or established, teachable methods. My process is completely intuitive. I don't know how I make decisions when I'm designing a quilt—I just do it based on years and years of making and looking at art.

I decided to try to figure it out, so I started to document my process while I made my next quilt. I wrote down every action as I worked. I wrote down tips and processes that I thought might be important. It was daunting and mostly irritating: I did it for the next quilt as well. But it was on the third quilt that it all fell into place.

I noticed I never sat down except at the sewing machine. I would put something on my design wall, step back to study it, make another something to place on the wall, step back to study it. The "pieces" I was using were often constructed units sewn from scraps in different configurations. I needed to find a descriptive name for these pieces and I decided to call them components. These involved cutting, sewing, and pressing. I was constantly moving between the cutting table, the sewing machine, the ironing board, and the design wall all day.

It just so happened that at this same time, I was busily exploring movement and dance. I listen to music all day in the studio and noticed I was dancing from workstation to workstation. The notion "Dancing with the Wall" popped into my head and the name stuck. It also gave me a working structure for developing my workshop and teaching practice.

Peppermint Twist

Limbo

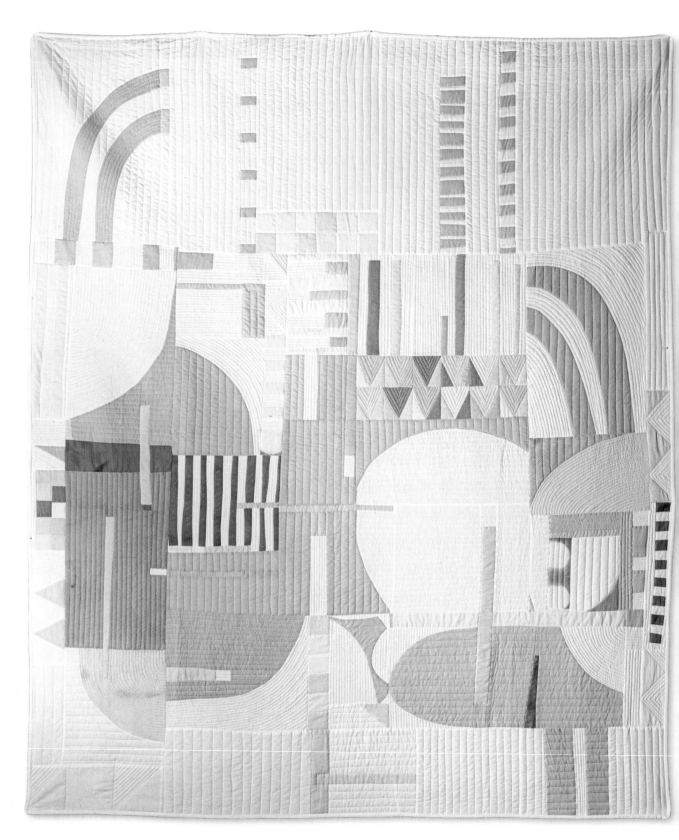

Gigue

I was busy working on the dance quilts during this time as well and "dancing" was on my mind! It's sad that I can't really dance. Too stiff and uncoordinated. I have included here several of my dance series: *Peppermint Twist, Woodcut, Limbo, Gigue, Dancing with Duchamp,* and *Flamenco.*

Woodcut

Dancing with Duchamp

146

IRENE'S QUILTS

Flamenco

The fabric dyeing led to experimenting with large pieces of fabric. I had seen some beautiful, deep blacks in quilts that were hand-dyed, and I wanted to use that deep, rich color in my work. The pieces I dyed didn't turn out very deep at all, but I loved the textures and patterns in them. I intended to use the fabric as raw materials for components, but when I viewed them on the design wall I knew I had to use them as the "ground."

So began a series of dark quilts. The first three in the series had pink cracks splitting the surface. The Me Too movement was in full swing and I envisioned women breaking through the wall of dark blue masculinity. These morphed into designs that played with light and color elements popping off the dark surfaces.

Around this time, I had an opportunity to revisit the Rothko Chapel in Houston, Texas and was once again overwhelmed by the power of the immense black paintings by Mark Rothko in the chapel. I freely admit the paintings were strong influences for these quilts. I quilted the dark quilts with varying width lines to try to signify his overlapping transparent layers of blacks, purples, browns, and dark blues. If you look closely, you can see this in *Cracks In the Façade* and *Pour*.

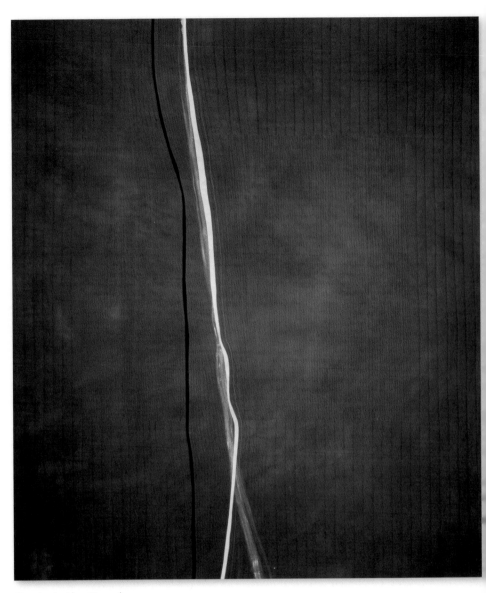

Cracks In the Façade

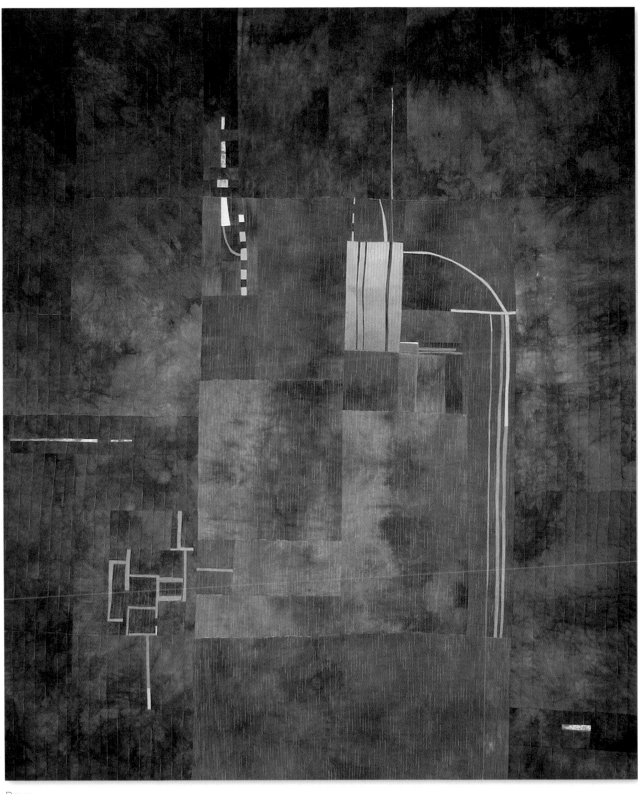

IRENE'S QUILTS

Pour

Spring Storm

IRENE'S QUILTS

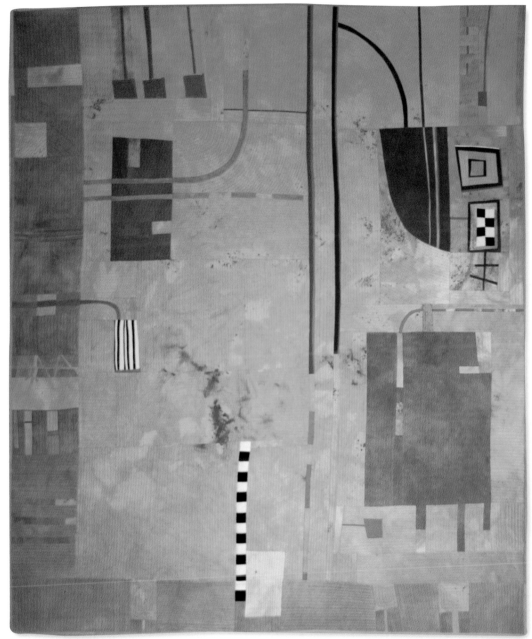

Green Eggs and Ham

Just so you know, my favorite color is chartreuse. I've renamed it "Irene Green" and prefer it to be a little dirty-ish. The Dharma Trading Company, a purveyor of everything dyeing, introduced a color of fiber reactive Procion dye called Green Eggs as a special color that I love! I dyed large panels of fabrics in Green Eggs with cooler greens to use as backgrounds for a new series of quilts, experimenting with blending the colors together and sprinkling dye powder on top of them. The patterns in the dyed pieces were very seductive and I couldn't resist making them into quilts such as *Green Eggs and Ham* and *Spring Storm*.

When I felt the dyed quilts were becoming stagnant and repetitive and that I had taken the dance series as far as I could, I started looking for a different challenge and another series to dive into.

The colorful quilts were fun, but not interesting to me anymore. The women's quilts were relevant, but too tedious. While working on the colorful ground quilts though, I was playing with skinny lines as a design element. It was fun to be able to "draw" lines through the surfaces by piecing in lines as thin as 1/8in wide. I wondered if I could actually make a quilt that looked like a pencil or charcoal drawing: I love drawing and it is my strongest artistic ability.

Curated Quilts magazine announced a black and white quilt challenge for an upcoming issue at QuiltCon 2019. I decided that a "line drawing" quilt would be a good way to approach the project. *Drawing In Black and White* and *Line Drawing Landscape* were the first two quilts in this series.

Drawing In Black and White

IRENE'S QUILTS

Landscape In Skinny Lines

I began to feel that, even though I was still making my quilts in exactly the same way as I had since I started Dancing with the Wall, the quilts were not turning out in the same vein.

Looking back, I think I was afraid that I was jumping from style to style and series to series without slowing down to fully explore each investigation. I had moved forward from the Dance quilt series because the colorful dyed fabrics distracted me—they moved into the skinny line quilts, but I was nostalgic for my former style.

I stopped everything else and made *Red Stripe* and *She's Lost Control Again*. I love the energy and exuberance of these quilts—they were a lot of fun to make and in many ways, they reenergized my practice. These were the last designs I made prior to my first Nancy Crow workshop experience. I knew the workshop would affect my style and was looking forward to working with my quilt hero(ine) and the opportunity to broaden my quilting skills.

Red Stripe

IRENE'S QUILTS

She's Lost Control Again

Voltron 1

IRENE'S QUILTS

Batik Voltron

As expected, the Nancy Crow workshop, titled Strip Piecing, was an amazing experience. Yes, by the end of the second day, I was in tears from exhaustion and just wanted to come home. We sewed from first light to long past nightfall. She pushed us by expecting nothing but our best work in a short amount of time. I thought I was well versed in art, but her focus on value took me by surprise. Needless to say, by the end of the two weeks of learning and sewing, I was thrilled with the experience and the new friends I had made.

I came home from my workshop with Nancy Crow laden with left-over strip-pieced fabrics. I was curious to experiment with how what I learned could be brought into my own practice. I started playing with the stripes and made a quilt that resembled the Voltron robot my sons had played with when younger. I loved the patterns the stripes made and was drawn to the symmetry of the quilts. Here are *Voltron I* and *Batik Voltron*.

John Prine

IRENE'S QUILTS

As much as I enjoyed making these quilts, and as much as others liked them, they weren't really "me." They didn't feel challenging enough to keep making strip stripes and putting them together in overall patterns. I needed to move on and/or (depending on how you look at it) get back to my own totally improvisational practice. The strip stripes that I hadn't used in the Voltron quilts still sat on top of my scrap bin and I found myself taking them out to use to begin my next improv quilt. I cut them into the same components I had always made from solid fabrics and started building a new piece. The strip stripes created complex patterns formerly unavailable to me. A couple of the quilts I made using the left-over strips are *Morg N Me* and *John Prine*.

Morg N Me

IRENE'S QUILTS

Then (cue scary dramatic music), Covid hit. Anxiety set in. Even though my life changed very little after shut down because I was already in my studio almost every day working alone and happy as a clam. However, the reality of forced isolation and fear of the political situation, on top of the possibility of contracting a deadly disease, made my life feel very different. Instead of feeling free and creative, I felt afraid and stifled.

It was hard to knuckle down and keep making quilts instead of watching television and pacing. I soon discovered that pacing and watching the tube are just plain boring, so I forced myself to get to work. I turned off and tuned out, and got back into my creative practice.

I've always believed, quite strongly, that when we let go and let down our guard, our deepest feelings pour into our creative work. I can look back at all my quilts and see the influences and thoughts that impacted them. The initial inklings of the depth of my anxiety appeared first in my "Illustrated" quilts and then my "Covid" quilts.

Mark Makers Spin

During the early days of the pandemic shutdown, an insistent mantra in my head was "we are all in this together." I started thinking about what defined us as humans as opposed to just animals. What sets us apart as a unique species? I think the impulse to leave our mark, to use language, to communicate, and to create as sentient beings holds the key.

I woke up one morning with an urge to start drawing on the quilt I currently had on my design wall. The piece was an uninspired attempt to keep busy and quell fears, and was the perfect canvas on which to experiment—I knew I couldn't make it worse than it already was! I grabbed the only permanent pen in my studio, a black Sharpie and started drawing. The act of drawing intricate patterns on fabric focused my attention away from the worries of the world. I liked the way my individual marks became a bespoke "print" fabric and reflected my individual marking style. Over the next few weeks, I ordered fabric pens that were acid-free and archival, and drew on many quilts such as *Complements, Floral Covid, Markings,* and *Corona.*

Complements

Floral Covid

Markings

IRENE'S QUILTS

Corona

Large circular objects started to appear in my quilts. They sat in corners and danced across the surface. They persisted in showing up over and over again: very stubborn things. It finally dawned on me that these had to signify the covid virus. I was bringing something that was microscopic into view so that I could see it, and deal with it. Soon, after there were talks of vaccines, funny looking chain shapes started interrupting the circles in the designs. These interrupters started getting bigger, taking out the covids until they were exploded in *Foggy Days* and *Covid Chaos*.

Foggy Days

IRENE'S QUILTS

Covid Chaos

Too Much Noise

IRENE'S QUILTS

Joe Meets Irene

The chain-shaped interrupters started turning into pointy spikes in *Joe Meets Irene* (some of the pointy shapes were made in a Joe the Quilter Cunningham workshop session) and *Too Much Noise*. The anxiety was reemerging more acutely as the pandemic continued seemingly without an end in sight, and the presidential election of 2020 loomed ever nearer.

Empty Speech Bubbles

IRENE'S QUILTS

As anxiety turned to acceptance and shut down turned into a new reality, my quilts turned to pale, delicate curves, dancing across a field of white. I'm reproducing graphite drawings in fabric. *Empty Speech Bubbles* and *Virgin of Willendorf* seem to be pulling me out of fear into tranquility and calm.

Venus of Willendorf

Celebration

IRENE'S QUILTS

The election is over and the world is cheering in November 2020. I made *Celebration* and it is the first in a series of quilts using hand dyed fabrics, circles, and thin lines in a different way. As I continue to explore these elements, the quilts have evolved into portraits of powerful entities that I call Guardians. *Best Friends, Guardian Royalty, Big Blue, Ghosts,* and *Guardian Ninja* are the first in the series.

The covid vaccine is becoming more available and the world is opening back up. I am continuing to work in my studio and look forward to what might be next.

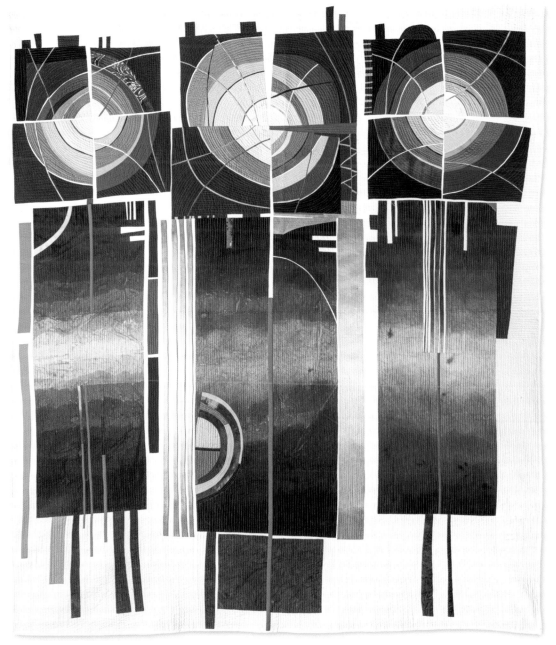

Guardian Royalty

Best Friends

IRENE'S QUILTS

Big Blue

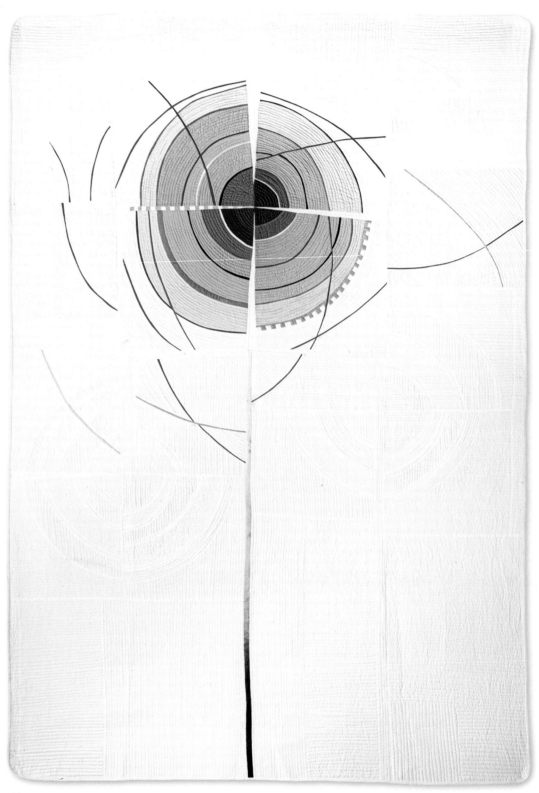

Ghosts

IRENE'S QUILTS

Guardian Ninja

SUGGESTED READING

There are thousands of books and websites and fiber artists available to us. I can't possibly find them all or even tell you which ones I've looked at and used in my quilt practice to date. So here are just a few that I have in my library:

For Improv

Grisdela, Cindy; *Adventures in Improv: Master Color, Design & Construction:* C&T Publishing, 2021

Grisdela, Cindy; *Artful Improv: Explore Color Recipes, Building Bloaks & Free-Motion Quilting:* C&T Publishing, 2016

Shell, Maria; *Improv Patchwork: Dynamic Quilts Made with Line and Shape:* Stash Books, 2017

Wood, Sherri Lynn; *The Improv Handbook for Modern Quilters: A Guide to Creating, Quilting and Living Courageously:* STC Craft/ A Melanie Falick Book, 2015

For Quilting

Cameli, Christina: *Free-Motion Combinations: Unlimited Quilting Designs:* C&T Publishing, 2021

Fons, Marianne and Porter, Liz; *Quilter's Complete Guide:* Dover Publications Inc., 2020

Gering, Jacquie; Walk: *Master Machine Quilting with Your Walking Foot:* Lucky Spool Media, 2016

Gering, Jacquie; *Walk 2.0: More Machine Quilting With Your Walking Foot:* Lucky Spool Media, 2020

For Color

Albers, Joseph; *Interaction of Color:* Yale University Press, 1977

Batchelor, David; *Chromophobia:* Reaktion Books, 2000

Hornung, David; Color: A *Workshop for Artists and Designers:* Laurence King Publishing, 2012

Thomas, Heather; *A Fiber Artist's Guide to Color and Design the Basics & Beyond*: Landauer Publishing, 2011

Wolfrom, Joen; *Color Play—Easy Steps to Imaginative Color in Quilts:* C&T Publishing, 2000

For Design

Barton, Elizabeth; *Inspired to Design: Seven Steps to Successful Art Quilts:* C&T Publishing, 2013

Doughty, Kathy; *Organic Appliqué: Creative Hand-Stitching Ideas and Techniques:* Stash Books, 2019

Marston, Gwen; Liberated Quiltmaking: American Quilters Society, 1997

For Inspiration

All books by and about Nancy Crow

All books by Gwen Marston

Arnett, *William; The Quilts of Gee's Bend: Masterpieces from a Lost Place:* Tinwood, 2003

Crow, Nancy; Nancy Crow: *Improvisational Quilts:* C&T Publishing, 1996

Cunningham, Joe; *Men and the Art of Quiltmaking:* American Quilter's Society, 2010

Kiracofe, Roderick; *Unconventional & Unexpected: American Quilts Below the Radar 1950–2000:* STC Craft/A Melanie Falick Book, 2014

Schmied Wieland; *Friedensreich Hundertwasser 1928–2000:* Taschen GmbH, 2014

I want to thank those of you who helped along the way. To Laura Morrison, the queen of details; to Lucinda Walker, the text editor and quilter extraordinaire; to Annie Hudnut and Patti Coppock, my partners in improv; to Ursula Foeller, Rita Mrozcek and Aleda Thweat, the Indigo Damen; to Jo Bryant, a most excellent book publisher-mentor. And, last but never least, to all of my students who have taught me how to put all this together through their hard work, enthusiasm, feedback and amazing contemporary improv quilts.